OECD
SOCIAL POLICY STUDIES

SOCIAL EXPENDITURE
1960-1990

Problems of growth and control

ORGANISATION FOR ECONOMIC CO-OPERATION AND DEVELOPMENT

Pursuant to article 1 of the Convention signed in Paris on 14th December, 1960, and which came into force on 30th September, 1961, the Organisation for Economic Co-operation and Development (OECD) shall promote policies designed:

- to achieve the highest sustainable economic growth and employment and a rising standard of living in Member countries, while maintaining financial stability, and thus to contribute to the development of the world economy;
- to contribute to sound economic expansion in Member as well as non-member countries in the process of economic development; and
- to contribute to the expansion of world trade on a multilateral, non-discriminatory basis in accordance with international obligations.

The Signatories of the Convention on the OECD are Austria, Belgium, Canada, Denmark, France, the Federal Republic of Germany, Greece, Iceland, Ireland, Italy, Luxembourg, the Netherlands, Norway, Portugal, Spain, Sweden, Switzerland, Turkey, the United Kingdom and the United States. The following countries acceded subsequently to this Convention (the dates are those on which the instruments of accession were deposited): Japan (28th April, 1964), Finland (28th January, 1969), Australia (7th June, 1971) and New Zealand (29th May, 1973).

The Socialist Federal Republic of Yugoslavia takes part in certain work of the OECD (agreement of 28th October, 1961).

Publié en français sous le titre:

DÉPENSES SOCIALES
1960-1990

After the OECD *Conference on Social Policies in the 1980s,* held in October 1980, and in light of the discussion of budgetary issues by the Economic Policy Committee, a Group of Experts on the Growth and Control of Social Expenditure met at the OECD in October 1983 under the auspices of the Manpower and Social Affairs Committe. The Chairman of the Group, Mr. R. Maldague of the Belgian Planning Commission, presented a report on the meeting to the 60th Session of the MSA Committee in December 1983. The Committee then recommended that the Secretariat prepare a report on social expenditure. After review by members of the Committee in July 1984, this report is published on the responsibility of the Secretary-General.

TABLE OF CONTENTS

Chapter 1

SOCIAL EXPENDITURE GROWTH: DEVELOPMENTS BETWEEN 1960 AND 1981

Chapter 2

THE DETERMINANTS OF SOCIAL EXPENDITURE GROWTH

Chapter 3

PROSPECTIVE MEDIUM-TERM DEVELOPMENTS

FOREWORD

The OECD Report on the *Welfare State in Crisis* (1981) identified the need for a systematic review by the OECD of the links between economic and social policies. Because economic policies have social consequences and social policies have economic consequences, it is essential that OECD countries seek to achieve their economic and social objectives through the coordination of both sets of policies. In particular the economic means to support a broad and flexible set of social programmes must be maintained, just as the programmes themselves must be effectively tailored to both social needs and limited resources.

The need for such a review grew out of an apparent conflict between economic and social objectives during periods of slow economic growth. Recent signs that OECD countries will be successful in restoring non-inflationary growth do not make such a review any less relevant. On the contrary, there can be no doubt that in OECD countries the length and depth of the recession, and the initially uncertain strength of the subsequent recovery, have served to heighten concern about this issue. If anything, a review of the links between economic and social policies is more vital now than a few years ago.

This report, which begins a series of OECD Social Policy Studies, is concerned with the growth of social expenditure, the determinants of that growth and prospective medium-term expenditure developments. Its principal conclusion is that, through the end of the 1980s, there will be little or no room for increasing the scope of the Welfare State. Although some improvement in benefits may be possible in some countries, the share of social spending in gross national product should not be allowed to increase; otherwise it could conflict with the aim of sustained economic growth. In a few countries this implies some further contraction, over and above that which has already taken place.

In a more optimistic vein, the study finds some comfort in the prospect that overall spending can at least grow in pace with real economic growth – a finding that contrasts with the dire pessimism about the Welfare State at the beginning of the 1980s. This nevertheless means that governments have at best only gained "breathing room" in which to prepare carefully for major reforms that will become urgent in the decade of the 1990s.

For the crisis of the Welfare State is not just a matter of financing existing programmes but of assuring room for new challenges that are in the making. As structural change, both economic and social, becomes a dominant feature of the OECD industrialised nations, new demands arise and their accommodation will put a premium on flexibility – the ability to adjust programmes in response to a range of social, demographic and economic pressures. Imagination will be needed if the Welfare State is to remain a creative instrument of modern society.

Reform of existing programmes and their better management can provide room, within projected overall budgets, for financing new developments. For this reason, further OECD social policy analysis will probe the problems of individual social programmes – health care and pensions, in the first instance – from both the economic and social points of view. There

7

may be scope for such major social programmes to offer considerably better value for money and to be more responsive to the needs of recipients.

If reforms, however difficult politically, are not put in place during the 1990s, governments and their electorates risk finding that they do not have the capacity or the willingness to provide social programmes adequate to longer-term demands.

J.-C. Paye,
Secretary-General of the OECD

INTRODUCTION

The growth of social expenditure, the share of national resources which it consumes, and the effectiveness and efficiency of social programmes are matters of vital concern for many OECD countries. Certainly, past growth of social expenditure has been rapid, outstripping that of national income throughout the OECD area. Social expenditure now averages about one quarter of gross domestic product. It is inevitable that such rapid growth should eventually have been called into question, although the passage of time would probably have seen some automatic moderation as the major social programmes approached maturity. In the event, economic developments forced a more urgent re-examination of social expenditure than might have been necessary if the strong economic growth of the 1960s had persisted through the 1970s and into the 1980s.

Economic growth slowed down abruptly following the two oil shocks of 1973-74 and 1979-80. This was accompanied by a greatly increased rate of inflation which in turn required a much restrained attitude towards reflation and recovery. In these circumstances economic and social policies were brought into apparent conflict. Social programmes appeared to have developed a momentum which was difficult to check, and this was being aggravated by additional demands for income support from a growing number of unemployed. At the same time, the exigencies of stagflation demanded the restraint of public expenditure growth and the reduction of government deficits. As far as the Welfare State and its material requirements were concerned what might have been an evolutionary social process began to assume aspects of an immediate budgetary crisis.

The OECD *Conference on Social Policies in the 1980s,* held in October 1980, provided a starting point for a systematic review by the OECD of the links between economic and social policies[1]. The papers presented at that conference and the ensuing discussion were largely aimed at diagnosing the nature of the crisis facing the Welfare State. However, the principal obstacle to successful diagnosis was incomplete knowledge about the past. It was clear enough that social expenditure had grown rapidly, but the forces which lay behind that growth and the relationship between economic developments, social expenditure growth and welfare delivery were not fully appreciated. Without a better understanding of these interactions diagnosis was difficult, and the move from diagnosis to prescription impossible.

The aim of this report is to provide this missing background detail, and thereby a better diagnosis of the crisis than was previously feasible. Some prescriptive analysis is also possible, although this is in the main left to other work dealing with the major sectors of the Welfare State, for example health, education, pensions and unemployment compensation. Thus in Chapter 1 broad developments in social expenditure growth since 1960 are described, and the major determinants of that growth are identified in Chapter 2. In Chapter 3 some judgement is made about prospective medium-term economic developments, and their implications for future expenditure growth are traced through. The object is to provide some perspective on the quantitative impact of the macro-economic constraint which growing social programmes will come up against. Chapter 4 attempts to draw some tentative policy conclusions from the preceding technical analysis.

The main source of growth in real social expenditure lies in discretionary policy decisions to increase programme coverage and real benefit levels. Demographic factors have been relatively unimportant. Nor will they have any significant expenditure implications in the immediate future. Thus, if no further attempt were made to expand programme coverage, prospective economic developments up to 1990 would be broadly consistent with continued increases in real benefit levels assuming no further increases in the share of social expenditure in GDP. This mildly encouraging conclusion has, of course, to be carefully qualified. The scenario implies significant restraint in relation to past experience: only a few countries have been able to stabilize the share of social expenditure in GDP in recent years, and the future increases in real benefit levels consistent with achieving this are very modest. And the idea that the scope of social programmes can be frozen may prove fanciful. The Welfare State has always had to face new challenges. These will continue to emerge, and there can be no guarantee that they can be met without further expansion of social programmes.

It must be emphasized that what is mainly being discussed in this report is the rest of the 1980s. However, some mention is made of problems which may lie further ahead, not so much in the 1990s, but in the earlier years of the next century when the post-war baby-boom generation begins to retire. Direct pressures on the Welfare State may be rather modest in the 1990s, but as pointed out in Chapter 4, the policies designed to meet the problems of population ageing may have to be in place by the end of the 1990s.

NOTE

1. The conference proceedings have been published under the title *The Welfare State in Crisis*, OECD, Paris, 1981.

Chapter 1

SOCIAL EXPENDITURE GROWTH: DEVELOPMENTS
BETWEEN 1960 and 1981

The purpose of this chapter is to describe the historical development of social expenditure in the context of the economic background against which it has evolved. For the moment, no attempt is made to identify the sources of social expenditure growth beyond the general influence of a changing economic environment and the economic policy responses which have been deemed appropriate.

The statistics on which this report is largely based are taken from OECD *Social Expenditure Statistics,* which are contained in Annex C. These statistics are compatible with and can be integrated into the OECD System of National Accounts (SNA). Most of the statistics come from published sources. In some cases it was necessary to ask individual countries to provide information not readily available to the Secretariat. National governments on occasions provided their own estimates when there were no data. The OECD Secretariat has also derived estimates where there was a basis for so doing; Secretariat estimates are clearly indicated in Annex C. Estimation was sometimes impossible, and as a consequence there remain a number of gaps in the statistics. These statistics are being continuously updated as additional data or better estimates become available; this report is based upon those available on 1st January, 1984. At that time consistent statistics for the period 1960-81 – with some gaps – were available for 19 OECD Member countries[1].

It is inevitable that some of statistics in OECD *Social Expenditure Statistics* are a poor indicator of the true SNA figures. This is unfortunate, though it is not necessarily a serious impediment. This analysis focuses on medium-term trends in social expenditure rather than expenditure levels at any point in time or short-term changes in expenditure. It is thought unlikely that the analysis has been much affected by any inaccuracies in the statistics used.

1. THE ECONOMIC BACKGROUND

A. Public Expenditure Growth

In 1960 the economies of OECD countries were about halfway through a period of more than two decades of unprecedented economic growth. These years were also the hey-day of the development of the mixed economy and the Welfare State, with the influence of government in almost all areas of economic and social activity becoming very considerably enlarged. Public sector growth was widely viewed as both a means and a necessary consequence of economic expansion accompanied by political stability. The public sector was in a position to divert resources away from the private sector, and redirect them to provide social

11

infrastructure. Through the creation of a wide range of redistributive mechanisms the State intended that the increased living standards which resulted would be shared by all groups in society. And fiscal policy instruments were assigned a central role in macro-economic strategies aimed at sustaining full employment.

The statistical picture for the period after 1960 is presented in Chart 1, which traces the year-on-year growth rate of public expenditure in the OECD area, the OECD area in this report being restricted to the countries for which appropriate social expenditure statistics are available. The situation in the seven major OECD countries – Canada, France, Germany, Italy, Japan, the United Kingdom and the United States – is highlighted in this chart and

Chart 1

THE GROWTH OF PUBLIC EXPENDITURE IN THE OECD AREA
1960-1981

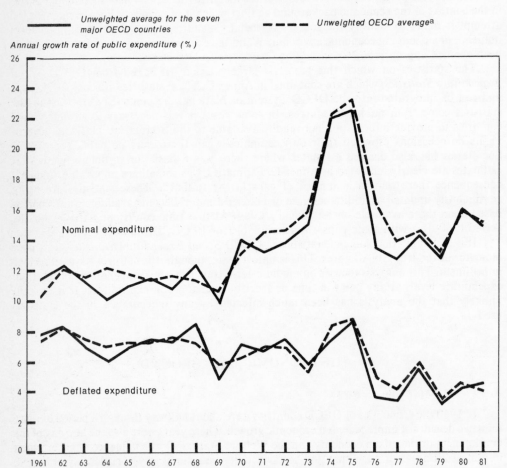

——————— *Unweighted average for the seven major OECD countries*   ‒ ‒ ‒ ‒ *Unweighted OECD average[a]*

Annual growth rate of public expenditure (%)

a. Average for 17 countries (excluding Denmark and Switzerland) except for 1961-65 (when Austria is also excluded) and 1981 (when Belgium and Greece are also excluded).

Source : OECD, Social Expenditure Statistics.

12

most subsequent charts and tables. Between 1960 and 1975 nominal public expenditure grew continuously though not steadily. There were two principal sources of expenditure growth. The first was the increase in public consumption. The second, and most important, was the increase in government transfers to households[2]. Public expenditure grew faster than gross domestic product (GDP). The growth rate of GDP is traced in Chart 2. The share of public expenditure in GDP increased from around 30 to around 40 per cent on average for the seven major OECD countries and the OECD area[3].

Part of the growth in nominal public expenditure reflects the general inflation of costs and prices. Between 1960 and 1975 the GDP implicit price index increased at an annual rate of about 5 ½ per cent on average for the seven major OECD countries and slightly faster on average for the OECD area, although at the end of the period costs and prices were increasing at twice this rate. Defining deflated public expenditure as public expenditure measured at constant GDP prices, it can be seen from Chart 1 that, like nominal expenditure, deflated public expenditure also grew continuously between 1960 and 1975, but its growth was

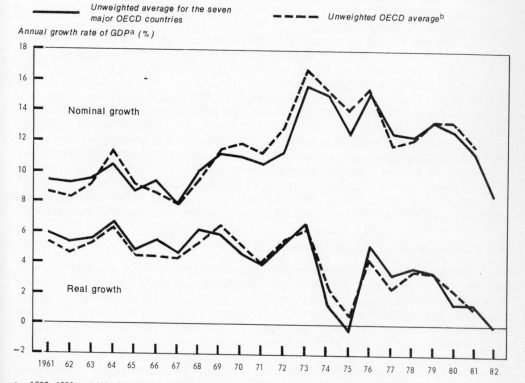

Chart 2

ECONOMIC GROWTH IN THE OECD AREA
1960-1984

———— Unweighted average for the seven major OECD countries   – – – – Unweighted OECD average[b]

Annual growth rate of GDP[a] (%)

a.   1982, 1983 and 1984 figures sometimes refer to real GNP.
b.   Average for 19 countries except after 1981 when the average is for the total OECD area.

Sources : OECD, *Social Expenditure Statistics* ; OECD *Economic Outlook* 34, December 1983.

13

steadier[4]. Real GDP – nominal GDP deflated using the GDP implicit price index – also grew continuously but, as Chart 2 shows, growth slowed down abruptly in 1974 and 1975. About half of the 10 percentage point increase in the share of public expenditure in GDP between 1960 and 1975 occurred in these last two years[5].

Despite an awareness that the growth of public expenditure could have been doing some harm as well as good, throughout this period the mood was one of optimism. The social and economic benefits of an expanding public sector, the equity gains which it was assumed were being achieved through redistributive measures, and the effectiveness of fiscal policy in maintaining full employment were hardly challenged. However, towards the end of the 1960s doubts were beginning to emerge about the efficacy of certain public programmes and about the effectiveness of fiscal policy itself. But, while often justifiable, in a climate of prosperity these doubts were not so compelling that serious questions about the role of the public sector had to be asked. They only became forceful with the major turnaround in economic fortunes which was to follow.

After the sustained economic growth of the 1960s and early 1970s, the mid-1970s brought severe stagflation, in the aftermath of the collapse of the system of fixed exchange rates, a commodity and food price explosion, and the first oil price shock in 1973-74. When indications of a permanent recovery began to appear, the consequences of the second oil price shock in 1979-80, reinforced by prevailing macro-economic policy, drew the OECD economies back into a recession from which they have only recently shown signs of emerging[6]. This more recent growth experience, as compared with that of earlier years, and the signs of recovery, show up clearly in Chart 2.

The relatively poor performance of the OECD economies since the early 1970s has been accompanied by some reassessment of the consequences of large and growing public sectors. The last ten years have seen a significant change in attitude. Rather than being widely regarded as a major contributor to economic growth and macroeconomic stability, the view that the growth and financing of the public sector has, on balance, stifled growth now attracts widespread support. Although it is recognised that the public sector still has beneficial effects, it is argued that these benefits cannot justify the damage done. Coupled with the view that widening government deficits foster inflation and impede growth, it is not therefore surprising that most governments have been attempting to restrain public expenditure growth. Chart 1 suggests that a measure of success has been achieved in this direction, although relative to the worsening growth performance this success must be judged modest. Between 1975 and 1981 the share of public expenditure in GDP still rose by 2-3 percentage points on average for the seven major OECD countries and the OECD area, and has continued to rise since 1981.

B. Public Expenditure and the Economy

There are numerous reasons why public expenditure growth, both in absolute terms and relative to GDP growth, is alleged to have undesirable economic consequences. On the expenditure side, it is sometimes contended that the current expenditure share is so high that the private sector of the economy has been squeezed into a position where it has to operate too far below its productive potential. This argument is then reinforced with the view that since there exists scope for efficiency improvements in the public sector, expenditure is higher than justified by the current range of public sector activities. It is suggested, for example, that public services are overmanned, transfer programmes are too wide-ranging, elaborate and open to abuse, and that the overall redistributive impact of government activities does not justify the resource flows involved. The activities themselves may also have undesirable consequences. Large state-run enterprises, income support programmes for individuals and

14

private industry, various forms of regulatory intervention, and tax expenditures and other off-budget activities place a limit on the influence competitive market forces can have on resource allocation in the economy as a whole.

The major source of finance for public expenditure is taxation (including social security contributions), and Chart 3 shows how, up until 1973, the share of total tax revenue in GDP increased more or less in parallel with the public expenditure share. Government deficits, also shown in Chart 3, remained modest although, in the seven major OECD countries, they were following a slight upward trend for much of the period[7]. However, the sharp decline in GDP growth in 1974 and 1975 gave rise to an abrupt increase in the public expenditure share which was not matched by as great an increase in the tax revenue share. Raising tax levels has never been politically popular, and is less so when real incomes are not increasing. Nevertheless, as Chart 3 shows, the ratio of total tax revenue to GDP continued to rise through the late 1970s, and 1981 marked the highest ratio in the majority of OECD countries. Fears that high levels of taxation blunt incentives to work, save and take risk, or that more widespread tax evasion and tax avoidance indicate that taxable capacity is close to being reached have been unable to prevent this. Indeed the same fears were voiced twenty-five years ago or more when tax burdens were much lower.

Nevertheless, because increases in tax revenues have not matched increases in public expenditure there have been large increases in government deficits since 1974, as shown in Chart 3, and these have persisted ever since. The initial rise was accompanied by a dramatic acceleration in inflation. Fiscal and monetary policy were therefore directed towards containing deficits as part of an anti-inflation strategy. These fell slightly, and a continuation of the restrictive fiscal policy stance and some further increases in taxation prevented any worsening of government deficits when the public expenditure share again rose sharply after the second oil shock. But government deficits remain much higher relative to GDP than before the first oil shock, and rising public debt to GDP ratios imply higher real interest rates which help to crowd-out private investment and stifle growth.

Whether the shift from optimism to pessimism regarding the economic impact of a growing public sector is justified has been and remains an open question. At the micro-economic level it is difficult to identify adverse effects of taxation and social security on labour supply, labour demand, saving or investment, although in some cases – for example, the tax-induced labour supply responses of married women and older workers – such effects can be supported by evidence[8]. At the macro-economic level, preliminary cross-country comparisons undertaken by the Secretariat have failed to reveal an inverse relationship between public sector size and economic performance as reflected in GDP growth rates, unemployment levels and inflation rates, or between public sector growth and inflation rates. However, the trend deterioration in economic performance in the OECD area is real enough, and so are large and growing public sectors. It may as yet be difficult to attribute the former to the latter, and those who do so may be forced to rely on arguments which are difficult to substantiate, but there is a ready willingness to adopt such a view, and in recent years it has been having a growing influence on economic policy.

The OECD area has moved from a prolonged period of increasing prosperity, through two recessions, and in 1984 appears to be experiencing some recovery. But it is doing so carrying unprecedently high government deficits. With large public sectors, high unemployment and a desire to cut taxation rather than increase it, these deficits could prove rather stubborn. It is against this background that the Secretariat's analysis of social expenditure proceeds.

Chart 3

PUBLIC EXPENDITURE, TOTAL TAX REVENUE AND GOVERNMENT DEFICITS
AS A PERCENTAGE OF GDP
1960-1981
(Unweighted average for the seven major OECD countries[a])

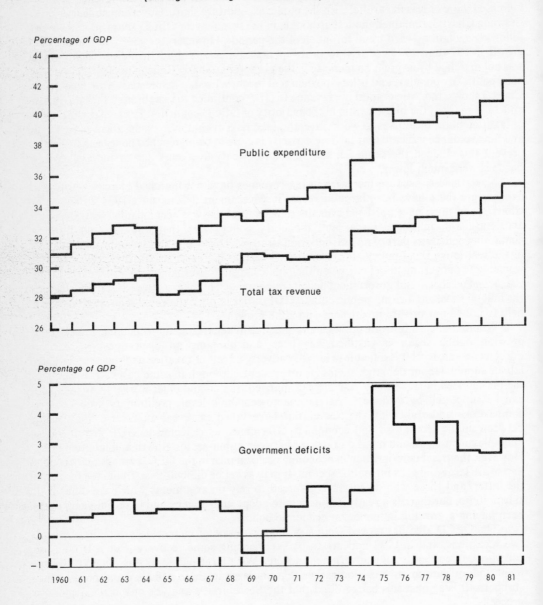

a. Averages for 1960-64 exclude Japan.

Sources : OECD, *Social Expenditure Statistics ; National Accounts of OECD Countries.*

Chart 3 (continued)

(Unweighted OECD averages[a])

Percentage of GDP

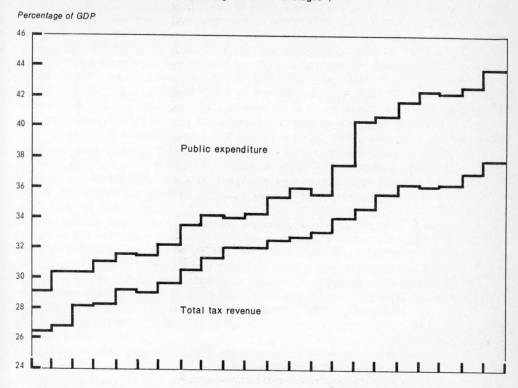

Public expenditure

Total tax revenue

Percentage of GDP

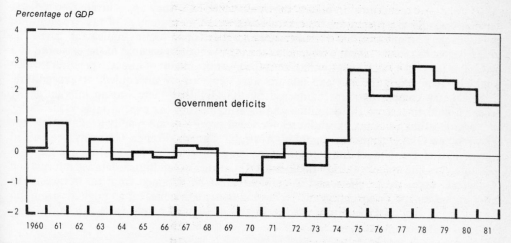

Government deficits

1960 61 62 63 64 65 66 67 68 69 70 71 72 73 74 75 76 77 78 79 80 81

a. Averages for 14 countries (excluding Denmark, Ireland, Netherlands, New Zealand and Switzerland) except in 1960, 1961 (when Japan, Austria and Norway are also excluded), 1962, 1963 (when Japan and Austria are excluded), 1964 (when only Japan is excluded) and 1981 (when Belgium and Greece are excluded).

Sources : OECD, *Social Expenditure Statistics ; National Accounts of OECD Countries.*

2. SOCIAL EXPENDITURE GROWTH

In this report social expenditure is defined as direct public expenditure on education, health services, pensions, unemployment compensation and other income maintenance programmes and welfare services. This does not represent the full extent of social expenditure in OECD Member countries. In many countries there are large private sectors in social provision – private health care systems and related insurance arrangements, private schools and universities, private pension, sick pay and disability insurance schemes – and flourishing charitable sectors. To build up a full picture of social provision would require detailed information about these sectors which at the moment is only available in part. Some of this is referred to in the related work on education, health and pension expenditures referred to above, but few references will be made to private social expenditure in this report.

The public sector's involvement in social provision is also greater than the social expenditure figures to be reported suggest. Many OECD Member countries have tax expenditure budgets which, even when appropriate accounts exist, are kept outside the realm of public sector accounting. Yet some tax expenditures, for example those which benefit families with children, are substitutes for direct social expenditure. Also the private and charitable sectors often benefit from generous tax concessions. These sectors are also regulated to varying degrees, and regulatory supervision is not costless. The failure to take account of tax expenditures is perhaps, on the surface, the most serious omission from this report, and it is therefore worthwhile explaining why it was decided to exclude them.

First, the magnitudes involved are probably very small, generally less than 1 per cent of GDP, and in the majority of cases less than ½ per cent. However, tax expenditures on individual social programmes may represent a significant proportion of total social expenditure on that programme, and exert a considerable influence over the public/private mix in social provision[9].

Second, there are challenging conceptual and measurement problems involved in attempting to estimate tax expenditures. For example, in some countries tax exemptions for dependants are regarded simply as part of the structure of a progressive tax system and are not therefore a tax expenditure. In others, they are treated as if they are equivalent to a direct expenditure, and are thus a tax expenditure. As to the measurement of tax expenditures, estimates can be made on either a "revenue forgone" basis or an "outlay equivalent" basis. The former refers to the tax revenue forgone by the tax authorities because of the existence of a particular tax provision. The latter indicates the pre-tax amount of direct expenditure which would be required if the tax expenditure were replaced by an equivalent expenditure. Cross-country comparisons are hampered by the fact that there are no internationally accepted guidelines as to the definition and measurement of tax expenditures[10].

Third, estimates of tax expenditures for social provisions are readily available for only relatively few OECD countries – notably, Australia, Canada, France, Germany, the United Kingdom, and the United States – and then only for selected years, although they are monitored in some other countries. In order to estimate tax expenditures, detailed information on income, taxes paid, reliefs and exemptions must be obtained from tax returns. The resources necessary for collecting and processing these data represent a major constraint on greater use of the tax expenditure concept in any subsequent extension of this work.

A. The Broad Trend

Chart 4 traces the growth of social expenditure in the OECD area since 1960. Social expenditure has been the fastest growing component of total public expenditure, its share in

Chart 4

THE GROWTH OF SOCIAL EXPENDITURE IN THE OECD AREA 1960-1981

——————— *Unweighted average for the seven major OECD countries[a]*   — — — — *Unweighted OECD average[a, b]*

Annual growth rate of social expenditure (%)

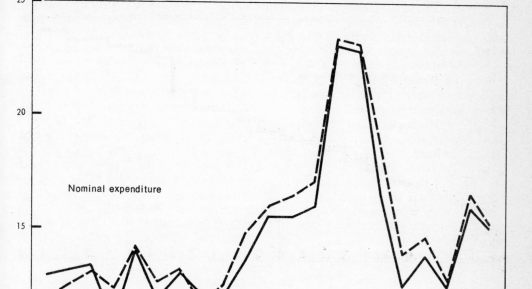

Nominal expenditure

Deflated expenditure

1961   1965   1970   1975   1981

a. Prior to 1975 there are no figures for expenditure on education in France. Therefore, only the growth rates for the years after 1975 reflect the growth in expenditure on education in France. The pattern of growth rates over these later years is unaffected by their inclusion.
b. Average for 17 countries (excluding Denmark and Switzerland) except for 1981 (when Belgium and Greece are also excluded).
Source : OECD, *Social Expenditure Statistics.*

Chart 5
SOCIAL EXPENDITURE AS A PERCENTAGE OF GDP
1960-1981

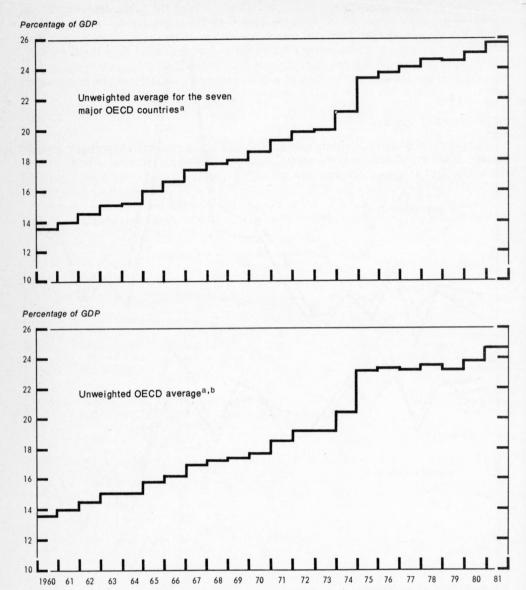

a. Expenditure on education in France is included after 1974. The breaks in trend are shown.
b. The OECD average is an average for 17 countries (excluding Denmark and Switzerland) except in 1981 (when Belgium and Greece are also excluded).

Source : OECD, *Social Expenditure Statistics.*

the OECD area increasing from 47½ per cent in 1960 to over 58½ per cent by 1981. Of the remaining categories – which include expenditure on administration, defence, law and order, housing and economic programmes – only the cost of servicing the public debt with recent high levels of interest rates and sizeable new borrowing has grown rapidly. As with public expenditure, the growth rate of deflated social expenditure – social expenditure measured at constant GDP prices – has been lower towards the end of the period than the beginning. However, as Chart 5 indicates, the share of social expenditure in GDP has kept on rising, and this is the principal reason why the share of public expenditure in GDP has also continued to rise.

B. Diversity of Experience

The pattern of social expenditure growth presented above appears to be straightforward. However, broad averages often give an appearance of clarity which turns out to be deceptive. Within the OECD area, although less so within the seven major countries, there is considerable diversity of experience. First, as Table 1 shows, there is substantial variation in the proportion of GDP allocated to social expenditure. In 1981 five countries – Germany, Belgium, Denmark, the Netherlands and Sweden – spent over 30 per cent of GDP on social

Table 1.   **Social expenditure in OECD countries**
1960-1981[a]

	Expenditure share		Annual growth rate of real GDP (%)		Annual growth rate of deflated social expenditure (%)	
	1960	1981	1960-1975	1975-1981	1960-1975	1975-1981
Canada	12.1	21.5	5.1	3.3	9.3	3.1
France	13.4[b]	29.5	5.0	2.8	7.3[b]	6.2
Germany	20.5	31.5	3.8	3.0	7.0	2.4
Italy	16.8	29.1	4.6	3.2	7.7	5.1
Japan	8.0	17.5	8.6	4.7	12.8	8.4
United Kingdom	13.9	23.7	2.6	1.0	5.9	1.8
United States	10.9	20.8	3.4	3.2	8.0	3.2
Average of above countries[e]	13.7	24.8	4.7	3.0	8.3	4.3
Australia	10.2	18.8	5.2	2.4	9.6	2.4
Austria	17.9	27.7	4.5	2.9	6.7	5.0
Belgium	17.4	37.6[c]	4.5	2.2[c]	9.3	7.9[c]
Denmark	–	33.3[d]	3.7	2.2	–	5.4[d]
Finland	15.4	25.9	4.5	2.9	7.5	4.8
Greece	8.5	13.4[c]	6.8	3.5	8.4	9.4[c]
Ireland	11.7	28.4	4.3	3.5	9.1	7.1
Netherlands	16.2	36.1	4.5	2.0	10.4	1.6
New Zealand	13.0	19.6	4.0	0.4	5.5	3.5
Norway	11.7	27.1	4.3	4.1	10.1	4.6
Sweden	15.4	33.4	4.0	1.0	7.9	4.7
Switzerland	7.7	14.9[d]	3.4	1.7	7.6	2.7[d]
OECD average[e]	13.1	25.6	4.6	2.6	8.4	4.8

a)   Or latest year available.
b)   Excluding education.
c)   1980.
d)   1979.
e)   Unweighted average.
Source: OECD, *Social Expenditure Statistics.*

21

programmes. Of these, only Denmark was not amongst the big spenders in 1960. At the same time, in two countries – Greece and Switzerland – the expenditure share was less than 15 per cent. These countries, along with Japan (where the expenditure share remains low by international standards) were also at the bottom of the league in 1960.

There has also been some variation in the pattern of social expenditure growth. Amongst the seven major countries Japan is at the upper end of the range of social expenditure growth rates and the United Kingdom at the lower end. Of the remaining countries Greece is at the upper end, and from the data available it seems likely that Portugal and Spain are similarly placed. These smaller Southern European countries have small but expanding welfare sectors supported by relatively high rates of economic growth. New Zealand is at the lower end of the range.

Slower economic growth since the mid-1970s and an accompanying response in the growth rate of social expenditure have been noted above. But again there are differences between countries in the relationship between the change in the growth rate of social expenditure and the growth rate of GDP. Table 2 shows the income elasticity of social expenditure for each country for the sub-periods 1960-75 and 1975-81. This breakdown of the full data period conveniently separates the later years of slow growth, large government deficits and expenditure restraint from the earlier years of growing public sectors

Table 2. **The income elasticity of social expenditure in OECD countries**
1960-1975 and 1975-1981[a]

	Income elasticity		Decrease in the annual growth rate between 1960-1975 and 1975-1981	
	1960-1975	1975-1981	Real GDP	Deflated social expenditure
			(Percentage points)	
Canada	1.8	0.9	1.8	6.2
France	1.6	2.2	2.2	1.1
Germany	1.8	0.8	0.8	4.6
Italy	1.7	1.6	1.4	2.6
Japan	1.6	1.8	3.9	4.4
United Kingdom	2.2	1.8	1.6	4.1
United States	2.4	1.0	0.2	4.8
Average of above countries[c]	1.9	1.4	1.7	4.0
Australia	1.9	1.0	2.8	7.2
Austria	1.5	1.7	1.6	2.7
Belgium	2.1	3.6	2.3	1.4
Denmark	–	2.5	1.5	–
Finland	1.7	1.7	1.6	−2.7
Greece	1.2	2.7	3.3	−1.0[b]
Ireland	2.1	2.0	0.8	2.0
Netherlands	2.3	0.8	2.5	8.8
New Zealand	1.4	8.8	3.6	2.0
Norway	2.4	1.1	0.2	5.5
Sweden	2.0	4.7	3.0	3.2
Switzerland	2.2	2.8	1.7	4.9
OECD average[c]	1.9	2.3	1.9	3.8

a) Or latest year available.
b) Indicating an increase.
c) Unweighted average.
Source: Table 1.

accompanied by the economic growth and taxable capacity to support them. The income elasticity of social expenditure is defined as the ratio of the growth rate of nominal social expenditure to the growth rate of nominal GDP. This is equivalent to an elasticity defined in terms of deflated social expenditure and real GDP, and the income elasticities of social expenditure reported in Table 2 are therefore derived from the figures in Table 1, as are the absolute changes in the annual growth rates of real GDP and deflated social expenditure between the periods 1960-75 and 1975-81 which are also shown. Table 2 highlights the inter-country differences referred to above.

In most cases the income elasticity of social expenditure for the period 1960-75 is nearer two than one; and in only six countries has the elasticity fallen to one or close to one for the period 1975-81 – Canada, Germany, the United States, Australia, the Netherlands and Norway. Of the seven major OECD countries, in the United States the elasticity has fallen significantly, the growth rate of deflated social expenditure having been more than halved with hardly any fall in the growth rate of real GDP. In Canada and Germany the social expenditure growth rate has fallen by two-thirds, but with larger falls in the GDP growth rate. In Italy, Japan and the United Kingdom the two growth rates have fallen more or less together, while in France the fall in the social expenditure growth rate has been relatively modest and the income elasticity of social expenditure has risen quite markedly.

Of the countries in Scandanavia and the remainder of Northern Europe, the elasticities in the Netherlands and Norway have fallen in a similar manner to that in the United States, the fall in the growth rate of deflated social expenditure in the Netherlands being remarkable. Of the other countries in this area, and of the remaining countries included in Table 2 (with the exception of Greece), Belgium, Finland, New Zealand and Sweden have experienced only a slight relative fall in the social expenditure growth rate with corresponding increases in income elasticities. Elsewhere, social expenditure growth has fallen broadly in line with economic growth, and income elasticities have changed little. The exception to all this is Greece, where the growth rate of deflated social expenditure rose despite a reduction in the growth rate of real GDP.

In the majority of Member countries the growth rate of social expenditure has come down. However, the shares of social expenditure and public expenditure in GDP have in most cases continued to rise, although more slowly than before. Against the economic background described above, it is not surprising that social expenditure has come under pressure. The fact that social expenditure continues to make an increasing claim on national income – as reflected in the expenditute share – will inevitably result in this pressure being increased. But a relevant review of social policies, and the ways in which they might respond to this increased pressure, cannot be undertaken at the level of total social expenditure. Rather, it is necessary to examine individual social programmes, and the forces which have determined their evolution.

3. TRENDS IN PROGRAMME DEVELOPMENT

An attempt is made to identify the forces underlying the growth of expenditure on the main social programmes in the next chapter. For the moment the practice of describing only broad trends, which has been followed elsewhere in this chapter, is continued. As is clear from Table 3, education, health and pensions have always been the largest programmes, in 1960 constituting approximately 78 per cent of the total and in 1981 80 per cent of the total on average for both the seven major OECD countries and the OECD area. However, there is variation in relative programme shares between countries. Worthy of note for 1981 are the

Table 3.   **Social expenditure programme shares in OECD countries**
1960-1981[a]

	Education share (%)		Health share (%)		Pensions share (%)		Unemployment compensation share (%)	
	1960	1981	1960	1981	1960	1981	1960	1981
Canada	24.8	28.8	19.8	26.0	23.1	21.4	12.4	10.7
France	–	19.3	18.7	22.0	44.0	40.3	1.5	6.4
Germany	11.7	16.5	15.1	20.6	47.8	39.7	0.5	4.4
Italy	22.0	22.0	19.0	20.6	32.7	45.4	1.2	2.4
Japan	50.0	28.6	16.3	26.9	17.5	27.4	3.8	2.3
United Kingdom	26.6	24.5	24.5	22.8	29.5	31.2	1.4	5.9
United States	33.0	26.4	11.9	20.2	38.5	35.6	5.5	2.4
Average of above countries[c]	28.0	23.7	17.9	22.7	33.3	34.4	3.8	4.9
Australia	27.5	30.9	23.5	25.0	33.3	29.8	1.0	4.3
New Zealand	20.8	23.0	25.4	24.5	33.8	37.2	0.0	2.6
Austria	11.2	13.7	16.2	17.0	53.6	49.8	1.7	1.8
Belgium	25.3	20.5[b]	14.9	13.3[b]	–	23.9[b]	–	6.9[b]
Finland	42.7	24.1	14.8	19.9	21.6	33.9	0.0	2.3
Greece	18.8	17.9[b]	20.0	26.1[b]	–	42.5[b]	–	2.2[b]
Ireland	25.6	25.0	25.6	29.6	21.8	18.3	5.1	8.8
Netherlands	27.8	19.7	8.0	18.6	32.1	36.0	1.2	2.8
Norway	32.5	22.5	23.9	23.6	23.9	29.2	1.7	1.1
Sweden	29.9	19.8	22.1	26.6	28.6	35.3	1.3	1.5
OECD average[c]	27.3	22.7	19.0	22.7	32.0	33.8	2.6	4.0

a)   Or latest year available.
b)   1980.
c)   Unweighted average.
Source: OECD, *Social Expenditure Statistics*.

relatively small education shares in Germany and Austria; the relatively small health shares in Austria, Belgium and the Netherlands (despite the share having more than doubled between 1960 and 1981); the relatively small pension shares in Japan and Ireland; and the relatively large pension shares in Italy, Austria and Greece.

There has been some shift in the balance between the major programmes since 1960, when the approximate shares of education, health and pensions in social expenditure averaged 28, 18 and 33 per cent respectively for the seven major OECD countries and 27, 19 and 32 per cent respectively for the OECD area. By 1981 these shares had become 24, 23 and 34 per cent and 23, 23 and 34 per cent, indicating a decline in the education share and an increase mainly in the health share. Expenditure on education and health grew much faster in the 1960s and early 1970s than in the remainder of the period. The growth rate of pension expenditure was initially less than those of both education and health. But thereafter it fell only slightly relative to general inflation while the other two dropped sharply, and in the late 1970s pension expenditure was the fastest growing component of social expenditure. In the years following the first oil shock it has been the welfare services of the larger expenditure programmes – education and health – rather than the pensions programme which appear to have borne the main impact of attempts made to control social expenditure growth.

Expenditure on unemployment compensation programmes has also been included in Table 3. This is a small programme, commanding only about 4.5 per cent of total social expenditure on average for the seven major OECD countries and the OECD area in 1981 (although twice that share in Canada and Ireland). Perhaps surprisingly, expenditure on unemployment compensation programmes actually grew faster on average prior to the first oil shock than subsequently, although the growth rate has always been volatile. Since 1979 the growth rate has again jumped, and it has subsequently been easily the fastest growing item of social expenditure. While unemployment continues to increase at recently experienced rates this should remain the case. Hence in the analysis of the sources of expenditure growth which follows, close attention is paid not only to the three largest programmes – education, health and pensions – but also unemployment compensation[11].

NOTES AND REFERENCES

1. The countries excluded are Iceland, Luxembourg, Portugal, Spain and Turkey.

2. A detailed analysis of the sources of public expenditure growth up to the mid-1970s is to be found in *Public Expenditure Trends*, OECD Studies in Resource Allocation, Paris, 1978.

3. These are based on figures taken from OECD *Social Expenditure Statistics*.

4. Deflated expenditure of course takes no account of price increases in the public sector which differ from those in the economy as a whole. These are discussed in detail in Chapter 2 of this report.

5. In this report, the share of public expenditure in GDP and the share of social expenditure in GDP – which will also be referred to simply as the expenditure share – is always defined in nominal or, equally, deflated terms. Much of the discussion in this chapter concerns the financing burden of public expenditure, and this is reflected in nominal shares. The concept of deflated expenditure – or expenditure in cost terms as it is sometimes known – has little intrinsic meaning, but when discussing how shares have changed in the context of economies which are growing in real terms it proves to be a useful expository device, and it also provides a convenient step in the analysis of expenditure growth which follows in Chapter 2.

6. OECD *Economic Outlook* 34, December 1983 and *Economic Outlook* 35, July 1984.

7. Taxation (including social security contributions) is not the only source of public finance. Therefore the tax revenue and government deficit shares do not sum to the public expenditure share. However, the other sources of finance, for example property income, tend to be small relative to tax revenue.

8. A detailed review of the evidence from a number of countries will be contained in a forthcoming report on the size and growth of the public sector prepared by the Economics and Statistics Department of the OECD.

9. One case where tax expenditures are relatively large is housing. Tax expenditures and other forms of indirect assistance (subsidies and rent control for example) have a significant influence on the structure of the housing market. Direct social expenditure – information on which is not included in this report – tends to be small and therefore to have only a marginal impact on housing decisions and housing market structure.

10. See *Tax Expenditures: A Review of Issues and Country Practices*, OECD, Paris, 1984 for further discussion of these issues and for a comparison of country practices.

11. The remaining programmes accounted for about 19 per cent of total social expenditure on average for the seven major OECD countries and 20 per cent on average for the OECD area in 1981. These shares have fallen by two percentage points since 1960. The major programme in this group is family benefits, which represented about a third of this residual share on average for the seven major OECD countries and the OECD area in 1981.

Chapter 2

THE DETERMINANTS OF SOCIAL EXPENDITURE GROWTH

In Chapter 1 the main trends in social expenditure have been described in only broad terms, so that the amount of information needed to convey twenty-one years of history of expenditure on the major social programmes in as many as 19 countries could be kept within manageable proportions. However, in order to turn a description of past trends into an assessment of likely prospects for the future, the more important elements which have made up the changes in social expenditure need to be identified and measured. This assessment can then form the basis for a review of strategies for social policy. In the present chapter the changes described in Chapter 1 are disaggregated within a statistical framework which is used to account for the various components of expenditure growth.

By itself such an accounting framework cannot provide any fundamental explanation of the changes which have taken place. The most deep-seated determinant of social expenditure growth must be a government's commitment to equity objectives – specifically social insurance, income security, the provision of merit goods, and wider redistribution – together with the prevailing judgement as to the extent to which these objectives can be pursued in the face of a trade-off between equity and economic efficiency. The strength of this commitment and the social policies which result are the outcome of economic, demographic and political developments as well as social ones. Some of these parameters are touched upon in the final section of this chapter and a more fundamental, but inevitably more speculative, enquiry into the causes of social expenditure growth is attempted in Chapter 4.

The growth accounting framework however has more limited objectives. It is not intended to analyse cause and effect. Instead its aim is to provide an exact decomposition of the growth rate of social expenditure - in total and by programme - in terms of the growth rates of a number of constituent components. *A priori* judgement suggests that the set of growth components used below highlights what are likely to have been the principal sources of expenditure growth. Although the decomposition does no more than partition an accounting identity, the influence of social policy changes, and their underlying motivation, need not be forgotten. It may not be possible to trace through the full expenditure implications of each and every policy change which has been implemented. But the general impact of significant shifts in policy stance between one reasonably extended period and another will often show up rather clearly.

1. THE ACCOUNTING FRAMEWORK

The change in expenditure on any particular social programme is by definition the product of the change in the level of service provided and the change in input prices per unit of service. The level of service should ideally reflect the output of social programmes. In the case of transfer programmes the output might reasonably be seen to be the standard of living available to retirement pensioners, the unemployed and other recipients of social security benefits, and this is something that ought to be measurable. However, quantifying the output of education and health services, and other public services, is fraught with difficulty, and the methods which have been tried have usually been found wanting. It is therefore far more common for the level of service to be measured by programme inputs. Thus levels of service in education increase as more teachers are employed, more schools and universities are built and more books are purchased. Levels of service in health increase as more nurses and doctors are employed, more hospitals are built and more medical equipment and drugs are purchased[1].

Changes in neither nominal social expenditure nor deflated expenditure necessarily respond to changes in levels of service as defined above, since they also reflect price changes. Nominal expenditure (E) is simply expenditure in cash terms, and therefore changes in response to general price inflation. Deflated expenditure (E*) has been defined as nominal expenditure deflated by the GDP implicit price index (D), i.e. $E^* = E/D$, and it follows that deflated expenditure changes in response to changes in the price of government services relative to the price of goods and services in general. Since, it is argued, there is limited scope for productivity improvements in the public sector, there is a tendency for public sector prices to rise relative to the prices of goods and services provided by the private sector, and therefore for both public and social expenditure to increase as a share of GDP. This tendency is referred to as *the relative price effect,* although the relative price effect as usually measured, and as measured below, tends to reflect both differential changes in productivity and unit input prices. Level of service, which is more commonly referred to as real expenditure (R), is given by deflating nominal expenditure on each programme by a price index appropriate to that programme (P), i.e. $R = E/P$. The changes in the ratio of the "own" price deflator to the GDP deflator (P/D) is a measure of the strength of the relative price effect.

The idea that account should be taken of increases in the price of education and health services relative to general inflation in determining levels of service is straightforward. The notion that cash transfers can become relatively cheaper or relatively dearer is perhaps a little more obscure. However, it should become clear once it is recognised that the standard of living of benefit recipients is a function of the prices they face as private consumers. Changes in nominal expenditure on transfers deflated using an index of consumer prices, i.e. real income, will provide some indication as to whether the standard of living attainable by benefit recipients is going up or going down[2]. Private consumption excludes some components of GDP while including items which do not contribute to GDP. The GDP and private consumption deflators therefore respond to changes in different sets of prices, and the relative price effect reflects this.

The description of social expenditure growth in Chapter 1 was in terms of expenditure, expenditure shares and income elasticities defined in nominal or deflated terms. Table 4 shows the real expenditure share (the share of real social expenditure in real GDP), the annual growth rate of real social expenditure and the real income elasticity of social expenditure (the ratio of the growth rate of real social expenditure to the growth rate of real GDP) in OECD countries. The difference between the figures in Table 4 and the corresponding figures in Tables 1 and 2 reflects the impact of the relative price effect. A comparison of the three tables reveals that this impact is in general small, and that it would therefore have made little difference to the broad description of social expenditure growth in Chapter 1 if it had been in terms of expenditure, expenditure shares and income elasticities defined in real rather than deflated terms. However, the relative price effect takes on greater significance when attention is turned to a country-by-country analysis of specific social programmes.

Table 4. **Real social expenditure in OECD countries**
1960-1981[a]

	Real expenditure share		Annual growth rate of real social expenditure		Real income elasticity of social expenditure	
	1960	1981	1960-1975	1975-1981	1960-1975	1975-1981
Canada	12.3	22.1	9.5	2.7	1.9	0.8
France	13.4[b]	29.1	7.5[b]	5.9	1.5	2.1
Germany	20.4	29.2	6.7	1.9	1.8	0.6
Italy	18.1	26.2	7.0	3.8	1.5	1.2
Japan	10.2	13.7	9.7	7.3	1.1	1.6
United Kingdom	14.8	23.1	5.0	2.5	1.9	2.5
United States	11.3	20.2	7.7	2.8	2.3	0.9
Average of above countries[e]	14.4	23.4	7.6	3.8	1.7	1.4
Australia	10.9	17.6	8.6	2.3	1.7	0.9
Austria	19.2	25.9	6.0	4.4	1.3	1.5
Belgium	17.2	35.0[c]	9.1	4.4[c]	2.0	2.0
Denmark	–	31.8[d]	–	4.0[d]	–	1.8
Finland	15.8	26.0	7.4	4.5	1.6	1.5
Greece	8.9	13.1[c]	8.1	8.8	1.2	2.5
Ireland	12.5	25.1	8.2	6.0	1.9	1.7
Netherlands	18.0	33.9	9.3	1.4	2.0	0.7
New Zealand	14.3	18.6	4.4	3.7	1.1	9.3
Norway	12.1	27.1	9.5	5.6	2.2	1.4
Sweden	15.9	33.5	8.0	4.0	2.0	4.0
Switzerland	8.0	13.9[d]	6.9	2.5[d]	2.0	1.5
OECD average[e]	13.7	24.3	7.6	4.3	1.7	2.1

a) Or latest year available.
b) Excluding education.
c) 1980.
d) 1979.
e) Unweighted average.
Source: OECD, *Social Expenditure Statistics*.

Real expenditure is the product of the size of the population relevant to a particular programme (N), the proportion of the relevant population which actually benefits from the programme (C) and the average real benefit received (B). These three components provide the core of the decomposition of social expenditure growth which is to follow. Of these, the first is largely demographic in nature, reflecting amongst other things the number of children, youths and young adults who can benefit from public education, the number of people exposed to the risk of ill-health, i.e. the whole population, the number of older people of retirement age and the total number of unemployed. The second component is to be referred to somewhat loosely as coverage, and reflects eligibility – the proportion of the relevant population which could potentially benefit from each social programme – and utilisation – the proportion of those eligible who exercise their right to benefit. The third component reflects the average level of service: real education benefits per student, real health benefits per covered person, and real income per pensioner, unemployment compensation beneficiary or other recipient of a social security benefit.

The components of the decomposition of the growth rate of social expenditure which follows have all been identified above. They themselves are to be presented as growth rates, averaged over two periods, 1960-75 and 1975-81. They are the annual percentage growth rates of:

a) *Nominal expenditure;*
b) The *GDP deflator,* reflecting general inflation;
c) Hence *deflated expenditure;*
d) Then *relative prices,* reflecting increases or decreases in the price of health and education services and the purchasing power of social security benefits relative to changes in the GDP deflator;
e) And hence *real expenditure,* which reflects –
f) *Demography,* changes in the size of the population relevant to a particular programme;
g) *Coverage,* changes in the proportion of the relevant population which actually benefits from the programme;
h) And hence *average real benefit*[3].

Terms in italics correspond to the headings in the tables which follow.

2. THE DECOMPOSITION OF SOCIAL EXPENDITURE GROWTH

A. The General Picture

A decomposition along the lines described above is set out in Table 5. This table refers to the average for the seven major OECD countries, and looks at only the four major social programmes. By setting out the relative magnitudes of the growth rates of the various growth components for a group of countries taken together it provides an immediate impression of what are likely to have been the principal sources of expenditure growth in the majority of countries. For the moment, a more detailed description of the way in which the individual country decompositions were done is set aside.

For the period 1960-75 the growth rate of real GDP averaged 4.7 per cent per annum across the seven major OECD countries. Comparing this with the growth rate of deflated social expenditure it can be seen that the income elasticity of social expenditure in general was around two, with some variation between programmes. Increases in education and health prices exceeded the general rate of inflation, although in both cases real expenditure still grew considerably faster than real GDP, an unambiguous relative expansion in the welfare services. Consumer prices increased at slightly less than the general rate of inflation, so that real expenditure under the pensions and unemployment compensation programmes grew a little faster than deflated expenditure. The share of social expenditure in GDP – the expenditure share in Table 4 – almost doubled between 1960 and 1975, with increases in each of the four major programmes.

For the period 1975-81 the growth rate of real GDP averaged 3 per cent per annum across the seven major OECD countries. Although the annual inflation rate was nearly four points higher on average over this period than over the previous period the overall growth rate of nominal expenditure remained much the same; the growth rate of deflated expenditure was therefore correspondingly lower. Only the growth rate of deflated expenditure on pensions stayed close to its earlier level. And only in the case of expenditure on education did the income elasticity of expenditure fall below unity. The rate at which education and health prices grew relative to the general rate of inflation fell, and consumer prices increased in line with GDP prices. The growth in real expenditure, particularly under the education, health and unemployment compensation programmes, was significantly lower than previously. The share of expenditure on each programme in GDP, except education, increased between 1975 and 1981, but only slightly.

Table 5. The decomposition of the growth rate of social expenditure 1960-1975 and 1975-1981[a]

Average of the seven major OECD countries

	Initial expenditure share	Nominal expenditure	GDP deflator	Deflated expenditure	Relative prices	Real expenditure	Of which: Demography	Of which: Coverage	Of which: Average real benefit	Final expenditure share
	1960									1975
						Annual growth rates (%): 1960-1975[b]				
Education[c]	3.4	14.7	5.7	8.5	2.2	6.2	0.6	1.4	4.1	5.8
Health	2.5	16.7	5.7	10.4	1.3	9.0	1.0	1.3	6.5	5.2
Pensions	4.8	14.1	5.7	7.9	-0.3	8.2	2.4	1.8	3.8	7.3
Unemployment compensation[c]	0.5	18.9	5.7	12.4	-0.3	12.7	4.4	1.5	6.4	1.1
Total of above programmes	11.2	15.1	5.7	8.9	0.8	8.0	1.6	1.6	4.6	19.4
Total social expenditure	13.7	14.5	5.7	8.3	0.7	7.5	–	–	–	23.1
	1975									1981
						Annual growth rates (%): 1975-1981[b]				
Education	5.8	12.5	9.5	2.7	1.3	1.4	-0.4	0.4	1.4	5.7
Health	5.2	14.3	9.5	4.4	1.0	3.4	0.5	0.1	2.8	5.6
Pensions	7.3	17.0	9.5	6.8	0.0	6.8	2.1	1.1	3.5	8.8
Unemployment compensation	1.1	15.7	9.5	5.7	0.0	5.7	6.5	-2.9	2.2	1.2
Total of above programmes	19.4	14.9	9.5	4.9	0.7	4.2	1.2	0.4	2.6	21.3
Total social expenditure	23.1	14.2	9.5	4.3	0.4	3.9	–	–	–	24.8

a) See individual country tables (Tables 6a - 6g) for details of years covered for each programme.
b) Average compound growth rates, calculated as the geometric mean of the individual country growth rates.
c) Six country average, excluding France.

Sources: OECD, Social Expenditure Statistics; OECD, Labour Force Statistics; OECD, Education Statistics Yearbook; SME education data files; Expenditure on Health Under Economic Constraints, OECD, Paris (forthcoming); SME pensions data files, and High Unemployment: A Challenge for Income Support Policies, OECD, Paris, 1984.

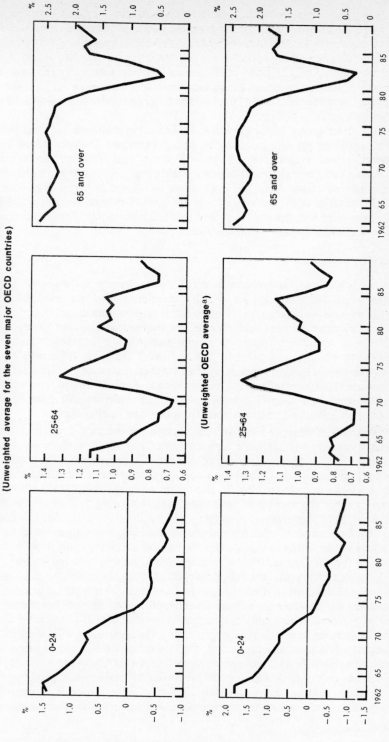

Chart 6

DEMOGRAPHIC DEVELOPMENTS IN THE OECD AREA
POPULATION GROWTH RATES BY AGE CATEGORY : 1960-1990
(Unweighted average for the seven major OECD countries)

a. Average for Canada, France, Germany, Italy, Japan, United States, United Kingdom, Australia, Austria, Belgium, Finland, Netherlands, New Zealand and Sweden.

Sources : OECD population data files and Secretariat projections.

In both periods the growth in total population was modest – around 1 per cent per annum up to 1975 and ½ per cent per annum thereafter – and its influence on social expenditure growth correspondingly small. However, changes in social expenditure did reflect a shifting demographic structure, and in particular the decline in the number of younger people in the population who could benefit from public education (see Chart 6). The coverage of all programmes increased more in the first period than the second, with health coverage hardly expanding at all between 1975 and 1981, and the coverage under unemployment compensation programmes actually falling.

The major determinant of the growth in real social expenditure has been the growth in average real benefit per person covered under each programme. Over the period 1960-75 this was 1 percentage point greater than the growth rate of real GDP per capita. Beneficiaries under the health and unemployment compensation programmes did somewhat better than others. As indicated above there has been some slowdown in social expenditure growth since 1975. However over the period 1975-81 the growth rate of average real benefits still managed to keep pace with the growth rate of real GDP per capita. Pensioners were the only group to fare significantly better than average.

B. Analysis by Country

It has not proved practical to provide a full decomposition of the growth rate of social expenditure for all the countries for which expenditure data are available. The ready availability of data on the coverage of the main social programmes is the major determinant of whether a full decomposition has been undertaken. Population data and unemployment data are available for all countries[4]. The age categories used to define the relevant population in the case of education (0 - 24) and pensions (65 and over) are fairly arbitrary. They are not intended accurately to represent ages at which a state education or a retirement pension can be provided, since this in part reflects eligibility changes. Rather they are supposed to be broad age categories which when applied universally across countries will allow the impact of general demographic shifts to be separated from changes in eligibility.

The number of children and students enrolled in pre-primary, primary, secondary and post-secondary education is available for most countries, although there are some gaps in respect of pre-primary and post-secondary education[5]. The proportion of the population either eligible for or receiving various categories of medical care under public health schemes is also known, although the data are patchy. In this report coverage is equated with eligibility for hospital care[6]. Either the number of retirement pensions being paid under the basic State scheme or the number of retirement pensioners who benefit from that scheme is known for 15 countries. And the number of unemployed people receiving unemployment compensation is generally available, although in many cases the number receiving some other social security benefit because they are not entitled to unemployment insurance is not known[7].

It will be clear from the preceding paragraph that the coverage data used in the decompositions are deficient in several respects. Coverage under a public health scheme for hospital care does not imply a stay in hospital, and medical care extends beyond hospital care. In the case of pensions, where only the number of pensions paid is available this may be different to the number of people receiving pensions (because some will be entitled to more than one pension). It is also important to note that the definition of pensions being used here is quite broad and extends beyond old-age pensions (see Annex C); in France in particular the basic state scheme only accounts for a small proportion of total social expenditure on old-age pensions, let alone pensions more generally defined. There is also a mismatch between beneficiary numbers and expenditure on unemployment compensation since in some countries

32

the expenditure figure includes the cost of benefits paid in addition to unemployment insurance, or in place of unemployment insurance when the unemployed are not entitled to it. While at any point in time these shortcomings imply that demography, coverage, and therefore average real benefit, are inappropriately measured, the fact that the analysis here is in terms of medium-term growth rates should reduce the impact of these measurement errors, although not eliminate it.

Tables 6a-6g present the decompositions for each of the seven major OECD countries. The main features which distinguish one country from another are summarised below. Particular attention is paid to changes as between 1960-75 and 1975-81. The decompositions for some of the smaller OECD countries are to be found in Annex A to this report.

Canada (Table 6a)

Canada is one of the three major OECD countries where the income elasticity of social expenditure has fallen from near two to below one between the two periods. In the case of each programme, except pensions, the growth rates of real expenditure and average real benefit have fallen significantly. This is particularly marked in the case of unemployment compensation, where over the period 1975-81 coverage has fallen faster than unemployment has risen.

France (Table 6b)

The lack of a continuous statistical series for expenditure on education and data describing the coverage of unemployment compensation programmes leaves the decomposition for the period 1960-75 somewhat incomplete. However, for the period 1975-81 it is worth noting that the annual growth rate of deflated social expenditure is high relative to the annual growth rate of real GDP, implying an income elasticity of social expenditure still in excess of two. This is true across all programmes except education, and the elasticity is particularly high in the case of unemployment compensation, where the growth rates of unemployment, coverage and average real benefit have all been well above average.

Germany (Table 6c)

Germany is the second of the major OECD countries where the income elasticity of social expenditure has fallen to below one, although it had less far to fall than others to reach this mark. The growth rates of real expenditure and average real benefit fell under each programme. In the case of pensions average real benefit actually declined during the period 1975-81, although coverage expanded.

Italy (6d)

The income elasticity of social expenditure fell slightly between 1960-75 and 1975-81, although only in the case of education was the growth rate of deflated expenditure higher in the second period than the first, largely due to a large increase in the relative price of education and health services. There was almost no growth in real health expenditure, and average real benefit consequently fell. Although the growth rate of real expenditure on pensions was about average, the growth rate of average real benefit was high, the consequence of a fall in coverage. The growth rate of real expenditure on unemployment compensation was high, as was the growth rate of average real benefit, the expenditure implications of an increase in unemployment being more than offset by reduced coverage.

33

Table 6a.   The decomposition of the growth rate of social expenditure in the seven major OECD countries
1960-1975 and 1975-1981

Canada

| | Initial expenditure share | Nominal expenditure | GDP deflator | Deflated expenditure | Relative prices | Real expenditure | Of which: | | | Final expenditure share |
							Demography	Coverage	Average real benefit	
	1960									1975
						Annual growth rates (%): 1960-1975[a]				
Education	3.0	15.9	4.8	10.5	1.9	8.4	1.3	0.9	6.1	6.4
Health	2.4	16.8	4.8	11.4	-1.4	13.0	1.6	2.6	8.4	5.7
Pensions	2.8	12.6	4.8	7.4	-0.9	8.3	2.4	2.8	2.9	3.8
Unemployment compensation	1.5	15.0	4.8	9.7	-0.9	10.7	3.4	0.1	7.0	2.8
Total of above programmes	9.7	15.0	4.8	9.7	-0.2	9.9	2.0	1.7	5.9	18.7
Total social expenditure	12.1	14.6	4.8	9.3	-0.2	9.5	-	-	-	21.8
	1975									1981
						Annual growth rates (%): 1975-1981[a]				
Education	6.4	12.0	9.1	2.7	1.7	1.0	-0.4[b]	1.2[b]	0.2	6.2
Health	5.7	12.4	9.1	3.0	0.0	3.0	1.2	0.0	1.8	5.6
Pensions	3.8	16.3	9.1	6.6	-0.2	6.8	3.3	0.4	3.0	4.6
Unemployment compensation	2.8	9.5	9.1	0.3	-0.2	0.5	4.7[b]	-4.9[b]	0.9	2.3
Total of above programmes	18.7	12.6	9.1	3.2	0.5	2.7	1.6	-0.2	1.3	18.7
Total social expenditure	21.8	12.4	9.1	3.1	0.4	2.7	-	-	-	21.5

a)   Average compound growth rates.
b)   1975-1980.
Sources: See Table 5.

34

Table 6b.   **France**

	Initial expenditure share	Nominal expenditure	GDP deflator	Deflated expenditure	Relative prices	Real expenditure	Of which: Demography	Of which: Coverage	Of which: Average real benefit	Final expenditure share
	1960									1975
				Annual growth rates (%): 1960-1975[a]						
Education	–	–	–	–	–	–	1.2	0.7	–	–
Health	2.5	17.2	5.8	10.8	–0.1	10.9	1.0	1.0	8.7	5.5
Pensions	5.9	13.8	5.8	7.5	–0.2	7.7	1.9	1.9	3.7	8.4
Unemployment compensation	0.2	22.5	5.8	15.7	–0.2	15.9	9.3	–	–	0.8
Total of above programmes[b]	8.4	14.8	5.8	8.5	–0.2	8.7	1.6	1.6	5.2	13.9
Total social expenditure[c]	13.4	13.4	5.8	7.3	–0.2	7.5	–	–	–	18.1
	1975									1981
				Annual growth rates (%): 1975-1981[a]						
Education	5.8	13.1	10.4	2.4	1.4	1.0	–0.6[d]	–0.1[d]	1.7	5.7
Health	5.5	16.6	10.4	5.6	–0.7	6.3	0.4	0.3	5.6	6.5
Pensions	8.4	20.2	10.4	8.9	0.2	8.7	0.8[d]	3.0[d]	4.7	11.9
Unemployment compensation	0.8	31.9	10.4	19.5	0.2	19.3	10.0[d]	3.5[d]	4.8	1.9
Total of above programmes	20.5	17.7	10.4	6.6	0.3	6.3	0.7	1.4	4.1	26.0
Total social expenditure	23.9	17.3	10.4	6.2	0.3	5.9	–	–	–	29.5

a) Average compound growth rates.
b) Excluding education and unemployment compensation.
c) Excluding education.
d) 1975-1980.
Sources: See Table 5.

35

Table 6c. **Germany**

| | Initial expenditure share | Nominal expenditure | GDP deflator | Deflated expenditure | Relative prices | Real expenditure | Of which: | | | Final expenditure share |
							Demography	Coverage	Average real benefit	
	1960									1975
				Annual growth rates (%): 1960-1975[a]						
Education	2.4	14.5	4.5	9.6	2.2	7.2	0.6	1.9	4.6	5.4
Health	3.1	14.0	4.5	9.0	2.3	6.6	1.0	0.5	5.0	6.6
Pensions	9.8	10.5	4.5	5.7	-0.6	6.3	3.1	-0.3	3.4	12.9
Unemployment compensation	0.1	28.7	4.5	23.2	-0.6	23.9	9.6	0.1	12.9	1.2
Total of above programmes	15.4	11.9	4.5	7.1	0.4	6.6	2.3	0.2	4.0	26.1
Total social expenditure	20.5	11.9	4.5	7.0	0.3	6.7	–	–	–	32.6
	1975									1981
				Annual growth rates (%): 1975-1981[a]						
Education	5.4	6.3	4.0	2.2	0.6	1.6	-0.9[b]	0.0[b]	2.5	5.2
Health	6.6	6.9	4.0	2.8	0.7	2.1	0.0	0.0	2.1	6.5
Pensions	12.9	6.6	4.0	2.5	0.4	2.1	0.9	1.4	-0.2	12.5
Unemployment compensation	1.2	9.2	4.0	5.1	0.4	4.7	2.9	-4.2	6.2	1.4
Total of above programmes	26.1	6.7	4.0	2.6	0.5	2.1	0.4	0.5	1.2	25.6
Total social expenditure	32.6	6.4	4.0	2.4	0.5	1.9	–	–	–	31.5

a) Average compound growth rates.
b) 1975-1980.
Sources: See Table 5.

Table 6d. **Italy**

	Initial expenditure share 1960	Nominal expenditure	GDP deflator	Deflated expenditure	Relative prices	Real expenditure	Of which: Demography	Of which: Coverage	Of which: Average real benefit	Final expenditure share 1975
		Annual growth rates (%): 1960-1975[a]								
Education	3.7	14.0	7.0	6.6	1.9	4.6	0.3	3.0	1.2	5.0
Health	3.2	16.4	7.0	8.8	2.0	6.7	0.6	0.9	5.1	5.8
Pensions	5.5	16.8	7.0	9.2	-0.4	9.6	2.6	0.3	6.5	10.4
Unemployment compensation	0.2	18.7	7.0	10.9	-0.4	11.4	0.1	4.8	6.2	0.4
Total of above programmes	12.6	15.9	7.0	8.4	0.9	7.4	1.4	1.3	4.6	21.6
Total social expenditure	16.8	15.2	7.0	7.7	0.7	7.0	–	–	–	26.0
	1975									1981
		Annual growth rates (%): 1975-1981[a]								
Education	5.0	26.6	17.5	7.7	3.7	3.9	-0.2[b]	1.3[b]	2.8	6.4
Health	5.8	22.0	17.5	3.8	3.7	0.1	0.4	0.2	-0.5	6.0
Pensions	10.4	26.2	17.5	7.4	-0.3	7.7	2.5[b]	-2.9[b]	8.2	13.2
Unemployment compensation	0.4	29.0	17.5	9.8	-0.3	10.1	6.7[b]	-8.6[b]	12.9	0.7
Total of above programmes	21.6	25.2	17.5	6.5	1.7	4.8	1.4	-1.2	4.7	26.3
Total social expenditure	26.0	23.5	17.5	5.1	1.3	3.8	–	–	–	29.1

a) Average compound growth rates.
b) 1975-1980.
Sources: See Table 5.

37

Table 6e. Japan

	Initial expenditure share	Nominal expenditure	GDP deflator	Deflated expenditure	Relative prices	Real expenditure	Of which: Demography	Of which: Coverage	Of which: Average real benefit	Final expenditure share
	1960									1975
		Annual growth rates (%): 1960-1975[a]								
Education	4.0	17.7	6.9	10.1	4.2	5.7	-0.2	0.4	5.5	4.9
Health	1.3	24.9	6.9	16.9	4.2	12.2	1.2	0.3	10.5	4.0
Pensions	1.4	21.2	6.9	13.4	0.6	12.7	3.4	4.2	4.6	2.7
Unemployment compensation	0.3	21.1	6.9	13.4	0.6	12.7	1.9	3.8	6.5	0.5
Total of above programmes	7.0	19.9	6.9	12.2	3.3	8.6	0.9	1.3	6.3	12.1
Total social expenditure	8.0	20.6	6.9	12.8	2.8	9.7	–	–	–	14.2
	1975	Annual growth rates (%): 1975-1981[a]								1981
Education	4.9	9.5	4.2	5.1	1.0	4.1	-0.3[b]	2.4[b]	2.0	5.0
Health	4.0	12.1	4.2	7.7	1.0	6.6	0.9	0.0	5.6	4.7
Pensions	2.7	20.3	4.2	15.5	1.6	13.7	3.7	4.2	5.2	4.8
Unemployment compensation	0.5	7.8	4.2	3.4	1.6	1.8	3.9	-6.1	4.3	0.4
Total of above programmes	12.1	12.7	4.2	8.2	1.2	7.0	1.2	1.7	4.0	14.9
Total social expenditure	14.2	12.9	4.2	8.4	1.0	7.3	–	–	–	17.5

a) Average compound growth rates.
b) 1975-1980.
Sources: See Table 5.

38

Table 6f. United Kingdom

	Initial expenditure share	Nominal expenditure	GDP deflator	Deflated expenditure	Relative prices	Real expenditure	Of which:			Final expenditure share
							Demography	Coverage	Average real benefit	
	1960									1975
		Annual growth rates (%): 1960-1975[a]								
Education	3.7	14.5	7.1	6.9	1.8	5.0	0.6	1.1	3.2	6.8
Health	3.4	12.8	7.1	5.3	1.8	3.4	0.4	0.0	3.0	5.0
Pensions	4.1	13.1	7.1	5.6	-0.3	5.9	1.6	0.9	3.3	6.3
Unemployment compensation	0.2	17.9	7.1	10.1	-0.3	10.3	6.5	-0.8	4.4	0.7
Total of above programmes	11.4	13.5	7.1	6.0	1.0	4.9	1.0	0.7	3.2	18.8
Total social expenditure	13.9	13.4	7.1	5.9	0.9	5.0	–	–	–	22.5
	1975	Annual growth rates (%): 1975-1981[a]								1981
Education	6.8	12.3	14.3	-1.7	0.3	-2.0	-0.4[b]	-0.5[b]	-1.1	5.8
Health	5.0	16.9	14.3	2.2	0.2	2.0	0.0	0.0	2.0	5.4
Pensions	6.3	18.3	14.3	3.5	-1.0	4.5	1.0	0.8	2.6	7.4
Unemployment compensation	0.7	29.3	14.3	13.1	-1.0	14.2	19.1	5.3	-8.9	1.4
Total of above programmes	18.8	16.2	14.3	1.6	-0.2	1.8	0.9	0.3	0.7	20.0
Total social expenditure	22.5	16.4	14.3	1.8	-0.7	2.5	–	–	–	23.7

a) Average compound growth rates.
b) 1975-1980.
Sources: See Table 5.

Table 6g. United States

	Initial expenditure share	Nominal expenditure	GDP deflator	Deflated expenditure	Relative prices	Real expenditure	Of which: Demography	Of which: Coverage	Of which: Average real benefit	Final expenditure share
	1960									1975
				Annual growth rates (%): 1960-1975[a]						
Education	3.6	11.8	4.2	7.4	1.2	6.1	1.1	0.9	4.0	6.3
Health	1.3	15.3	4.2	10.8	0.4	10.3	1.2	4.1	4.7	3.7
Pensions	4.2	11.3	4.2	6.9	-0.3	7.2	2.1	2.9	2.0	6.9
Unemployment compensation	0.6	12.5	4.2	7.9	-0.3	8.3	4.9	1.0	2.2	1.2
Total of above programmes	9.7	12.1	4.2	7.7	0.4	7.3	1.8	2.2	3.1	18.1
Total social expenditure	10.9	12.5	4.2	8.0	0.3	7.7	—	—	—	20.8
	1975									1981
				Annual growth rates (%): 1975-1981[a]						
Education	6.3	8.6	7.8	0.7	0.3	0.4	-0.2[b]	-1.3[b]	1.9	5.5
Health	3.7	13.9	7.8	5.7	1.8	3.8	1.0	0.0	2.8	4.2
Pensions	6.9	12.5	7.8	4.5	0.0	4.4	2.5	0.7	1.1	7.4
Unemployment compensation	1.2	-2.3	7.8	-9.5	0.0	-9.5	-0.7[b]	-4.2[b]	-4.9	0.5
Total of above programmes	18.1	10.4	7.8	2.5	0.5	2.0	1.1	0.5	1.3	17.6
Total social expenditure	20.8	11.2	7.8	3.2	0.4	2.8	—	—	—	20.8

a) Average compound growth rates.
b) 1975-1980.
Sources: See Table 5.

40

Japan (Table 6e)

The share of social expenditure in GDP in Japan has in the past been low, but a relatively high growth rate of social expenditure relative to GDP growth has pulled it slightly nearer the average. The growth rates of real social expenditure and average real benefit remained high through the 1960s and 1970s, although there has been a slowdown over later years except in the case of pensions, where the elderly population and pension coverage have both been growing relatively quickly.

United Kingdom (Table 6f)

Despite a marked reduction in the growth rate of real social expenditure, the income elasticity remained relatively high, a consequence of very poor growth performance over the later period. The education programme has been in marked decline, while the unemployment compensation programme has grown relatively quickly. Unemployment has been growing and although the impact of increased coverage has been more then nullified by a sharp fall in average real benefit, the growth rate of real expenditure has been high.

United States (6g)

The United States is the third of the major OECD countries in which the income elasticity of social expenditure has fallen to one, in this case from above 2, despite only a modest decline in growth performance. The growth rates of real expenditure and average real benefit have fallen for each programme, markedly in the case of unemployment compensation, which is the only programme where average real benefit also fell.

3. ANALYSIS BY PROGRAMME

Comparing the two periods 1960-75 and 1975-81, the growth rates of real expenditure on education, health and unemployment compensation were, in general, much lower during the second period, while growth fell only slightly for pensions. If these changes can to a significant degree be regarded as the outcome of policy responses to the economic pressures described in Chapter 1, education, health and unemployment compensation programmes appear to have borne the brunt of attempts to control expenditure growth while the pensions programme has escaped fairly lightly. Part of this difference is of course explained by the differential influence of demographic factors. But, taken together, changes in programme coverage and average real benefits have had a much greater impact on expenditure growth, and an element of control can be exerted over both coverage rates and levels of service. The purpose of this section is to provide some additional observations on developments in each of the four programmes distinguished above. These observations are intended to provide some amplification and further insight into both the endogenous and exogenous influences on the growth of expenditure on each of the programmes.

A. Education

Public expenditure on education grew rapidly during the 1960s and early 1970s, and a large part of this expansion derived from increases in enrolments and increases in the quantity of education services provided for each student. Developments in public education over this period comprised mainly the extension and reinforcement of the existing educational structure. The range and choice of academic and technical subjects was widened. The span of compulsory schooling was increased from 5 or 6 years to 9 or even 10 years. Pre-primary schooling was encouraged, both as a response to an increasing demand by working wives and as an early introduction to schooling which was particularly important for children from less-advantaged socio-economic backgrounds. At the other end of the system, higher education expanded very rapidly, first the universities and later other higher education institutions. Post-compulsory secondary schooling expanded equally rapidly, partly as a pre-requisite for higher education, partly in its own right as a qualification for entry into the upper sections of the non-professional work force. Teacher numbers grew more than proportionately, the ratio of students to teachers was reduced at all levels of education, and the growth of both student and teacher numbers was associated with a substantial increase in the education building programme.

Throughout this period the population of compulsory school age increased, reaching peak growth rates in the mid- to late-1960s (except in Japan). From the beginning of the 1970s numbers began to decline (again with Japan as the principal exception). Enrolments also fell, although enrolment rates tended to rise, substantially in the case of pre-primary and higher education. This was probably a response to increasing labour force participation by women and worsening unemployment, particularly towards the end of the period. The growth of education expenditure nevertheless slackened, partly a consequence of demographic developments and partly a consequence of tighter expenditure policies. The latter tended to be directed towards capital expenditure rather than current expenditure. Indeed, it is interesting to note that the ratio of students to teachers, which fell through the 1960s and 1970s, continued to fall in the late 1970s in those countries for which information is available, and only began to show signs of a reversal in the early 1980s.

B. Health

Public expenditure on health also grew rapidly during the 1960s and early 1970s. During the 1960s public health programmes were still expanding their coverage of the population. Although most of the population in OECD countries possessed free access to hospital care by 1960 (the main exception being the United States) coverage for other health benefits was more limited. The decade which followed was marked by the introduction of major public programmes in a number of countries and by the extension of existing programmes in others. By the early 1970s, however, this movement had lost most of its force, either because countries were approaching almost universal coverage or, in those countries where private expenditure still played an important part in the provision of health services, because of the development of private sector insurance schemes.

While the growth rate of coverage slowed down, advances in medical technology provided a continually increasing demand for medical services, and in the majority of cases this demand could be justified by reference to the success of medical innovations in a variety of fields. The widespread application of best-practice technologies has seen the incidence and consequencies of infectious and parasitic diseases severely reduced; expectancy of life in good health increased; and the life expectancy and quality of life of the infirm, disabled and mentally-ill much improved.

In many countries conscious attempts have been made to control the growth of health expenditure, and real expenditures and average real benefit have in recent years grown much more slowly than previously. But, it is likely that the measured reductions in the growth rate of real expenditure overstate what has happened to levels of service actually provided, since productivity increases and, in particular, quality changes are not fully reflected in health price indices.

C. Pensions

In contrast to the other major items of social expenditure, expenditure on pensions has in general not grown at a significantly slower rate over the 1975-81 period compared to the 1960-75 period. Even though the elderly population has been increasing in size relative to the population as a whole, pension coverage has continued to expand, and so have average real benefits. Given that pension programmes are so large, and given the pressure to bring the growth of social expenditure under control, it is perhaps surprising that expenditure on these programmes is still growing fairly quickly. It is the long-term contractual nature of old-age pension commitments which makes this fairly inevitable, at least in the short to medium term.

It is sometimes argued that there is an implicit inter-generational contract underlying public old-age pension arrangements, under the terms of which each working generation, through the intermediary of the government, provides pensions for the retired generation. Whatever the force of this contract, it has in general been honoured by the young and implemented by governments; as a result, only a small measure of control over pension expenditure has proved possible. Some flexibility has been provided by the indexation payments made to compensate for the erosion in the real value of the past earnings on which pensions are often based, and of pensions themselves, brought about by inflation. A handful of countries changed their indexation procedures in the mid- to late-1970s. But, indexation is an important element in the pension contract, particularly at higher rates of inflation, and only where there was already a large element of over-indexation – as in Germany and the United States – has expenditure growth been curtailed to any significant degree. Elsewhere, it proved difficult to make much of an impression on expenditure growth by this means, or by any other adjustments to the pension formula.

D. Unemployment Compensation

Expenditure on unemployment compensation programmes grew fairly rapidly over the period 1960-75, mainly as a result of increasingly generous benefits. Since 1975 the growth rate has declined despite the increase in the unemployment rate for the OECD area from 5.2 per cent in 1975 to 6.7 per cent in 1981; this was largely because coverage declined[8]. This has resulted partly from policy decisions to introduce more stringent eligibility criteria, but it is also a reflection of changes in the composition of the unemployed, with those less likely to be eligible for unemployment compensation – youths, married women and the long-term unemployed – forming an increasingly large share of the total. Unemployment insurance is designed for the short-term unemployed with some history of previous employment. Those unemployed not in receipt of an insurance benefit will usually receive some other social security benefit in its place. Some may be eligible for a retirement pension, and therefore part of the increase in expenditure on benefits for the unemployed shows up as an increase in pension expenditure. But most will move on to whatever scheme provides the safety net in a particular country, which in expenditure terms is in some countries treated as unemployment compensation but in others is simply combined with welfare assistance payments made to other groups of people in need who do not qualify for a social security benefit linked specifically to a contingency which gives rise to need, for example retirement, sickness, disability or unemployment.

NOTES AND REFERENCES

1. In some countries *ad hoc* adjustments are made to reflect the impact of increases in public sector productivity on public sector output. See T.P. Hill, *The Measurement of Real Product,* OECD, Paris, 1971 for details of the practices in these countries.

2. Attained standards of living are reflected in actual consumption, that is the value of all goods and services consumed in a particular period. Changes in income, and even expenditure, are poor proxies for changes in consumption and, thereby, attained standards of living. But changes in income will be a much better proxy for changes in potential consumption and therefore attainable standards of living.

3. For a period of T years these growth rates are given by:

   a) Nominal expenditure $[(E_T/E_0)^{1/T} - 1]$ 100 %

   b) GDP deflator $[(D_T/D_0)^{1/T} - 1]$ 100 %

   c) Deflated expenditure $- [(E_T/E_0 . D_0/D_T)^{1/T} - 1]$ 100 %
   $$= [(E_T^*/E_0^*)^{1/T} - 1] \ 100 \%$$

   d) Relative prices $[(P_T/P_0 . D_0/D_T)^{1/T} - 1]$ 100 %

   e) Real expenditure $[(E_T/E_0 . P_0/P_T)^{1/T} - 1]$ 100 %
   $$= [(R_T/R_0)^{1/T} - 1] \ 100 \%$$

   f) Demography $[(N_T/N_0)^{1/T} - 1]$ 100 %

   g) Coverage $[(C_T/C_0)^{1/T} - 1]$ 100 %

   h) Average real benefit $[(R_T/R_0 . C_0/C_T . N_0/N_T)^{1/T} - 1]$ 100 %
   $$= [(B_T/B_0)^{1/T} - 1] \ 100 \%$$

   Decompositions of this type were pioneered by the OECD Secretariat. See *Public Expenditure on Income Maintenance Programmes* (1976), *Public Expenditure on Education* (1976), *Public Expenditure on Health* (1977), and *Public Expenditure Trends* (1978), OECD Studies in Resource Allocation, OECD, Paris.

4. Population data are taken from data files maintained by the Directorate for Social Affairs, Manpower and Education (SME) and unemployment data from OECD *Labour Force Statistics.*

5. Enrolment data for the period prior to 1975 are taken from the OECD *Education Statistics Yearbook,* 1974; for the period from 1975 data are taken from SME education data files.

6. Data on coverage under public health schemes are taken from *Expenditure on Health Under Economic Constraints,* OECD, Paris (forthcoming). There are not sufficient data to estimate the proportion of the population which consumes some sort of medical service. The data on hospital care are better – more accurate and more complete – than those on other medical services.

7. The data on coverage under public old-age pension schemes are taken from individual country sources which will be listed in a forthcoming publication on pensions. Data are maintained on file for the seven major OECD countries plus Australia, Denmark, Finland, Ireland, the Netherlands, New Zealand, Norway and Sweden. The data on coverage under unemployment compensation schemes for the seven major OECD countries are taken from *High Unemployment: A Challenge for Income Support Policies,* OECD, Paris, 1984. Some additional data are taken from the sources cited therein, and data for most of the other countries listed above have been obtained from individual country sources mention of which accompanies the tables where the data are used.

8. OECD *Employment Outlook,* September 1983.

Chapter 3

PROSPECTIVE MEDIUM-TERM DEVELOPMENTS

The purpose of this chapter is to use the historical analysis of social expenditure growth as the basis for a view about developments up to 1990. The future growth of social expenditure, and the pressures to which this growth might give rise, are inextricably linked with parallel economic developments. By focusing attention on the medium-term, the discussion avoids the immediate issues surrounding cyclical disturbance and adjustment. It also avoids some of the longer-term problems, particularly those associated with ageing populations. But even the more limited exercise which results from the exclusion of longer-term considerations remains speculative because the range of reasonably likely economic outcomes in the medium term is large.

Despite the uncertainty, some assessment of future economic prospects has to be made. In this report, reliance is placed on an illustrative scenario which takes as its starting point the short-term forecast published by the OECD Secretariat in December 1983[1]. The future could, of course, turn out to be more or less favourable than this scenario suggests. But it nonetheless provides a useful benchmark against which to assess the implications of the evolving forces which will lie behind social expenditure growth – and in particular demographic change – in the context of the economic developments which could accompany these forces over the remainder of the decade.

1. ECONOMIC DEVELOPMENTS TO 1990

During 1983 economic activity increased in most OECD countries, reflecting the strong growth in the United States. In its December 1983 short-term forecast the OECD Secretariat predicted a continuation of the recovery in the OECD area through 1984 and into the first half of 1985.

In order to construct the illustrative scenario for the period 1981-90 an informal projection takes over from the short-term forecast in the second half of 1985 [2]. The broad features of the projection are not dissimilar to those emerging in the 1984-85 period. There is some further convergence of growth rates beyond that indicated in the short-term forecast. Unemployment continues to fall in the United States, but there is little change elsewhere, except in the case of some smaller countries where a significant increase in the unemployment rate is projected. Inflation stabilizes throughout the OECD area[3].

When compared with the period 1975-81, the scenario for the period 1981-90 is fairly gloomy. Despite the recovery, projected growth rates are generally lower in the second period than those achieved in the late 1970s. With the exception of Japan and the United States, unemployment rates in 1990, as in 1984, will continue to be higher than in 1981. In Europe as a whole there is a tendency for unemployment to grow beyond the historically high rates recorded in 1984. Inflation rates are, however, somewhat lower than previously.

2. THE IMPLICATIONS OF ECONOMIC DEVELOPMENTS FOR SOCIAL EXPENDITURE

Projected economic developments have two types of implication for social expenditure. First they have a direct influence on the growth rate of real expenditure. For example, *ceteris paribus*, real expenditure on unemployment compensation programmes will be determined by the projected level of unemployment. Second, economic developments have an indirect influence on future levels of expenditure. This operates through the pressures set up when projected social expenditure growth and the capacity of the economy to support it appear to come into conflict. The purpose of this section is to investigate the likelihood of such conflict emerging before 1990.

As outlined in Chapter 1, the presence or absence of conflict between social and economic objectives is partly a matter of public and government attitudes to the size and growth of the public sector. If circumstances combine to suggest an increase in the share of social expenditure in GDP, this may be viewed as producing a conflict for a government which has a stated commitment to the expansion of the private sector of the economy and to reducing the burden of taxation. Another government may be willing to let the social expenditure share increase, reflecting its belief that such an option can be pursued without coming up against any economic constraint.

To translate projected economic developments into a view about the growth of social expenditure clearly requires that some assumption be made about policy intent. Based on the evidence of recent years it is fair to assume that a number of Member country governments now accept that some limitation should be placed on the growth of social expenditure relative to the growth of GDP. If this policy stance is adopted, an assumption can be made about the income elasticity of social expenditure that governments are prepared to adopt. Then, in the light of projected economic and demographic developments, the impact of this assumption for social expenditure growth between the base year and 1990 can be estimated. Such an approach effectively regards the future provision of welfare services and social security benefits as being determined by the supply of economic resources.

Alternatively, some assumptions could be made about the future demand for welfare services and social security benefits, based partly on broad and rather general ideas about social needs and their political acceptability. The implications of these assumptions for the change in the share of social expenditure in GDP can then be traced through. The results of either of these approaches can of course be inferred from the other, although there is some expositive advantage in reporting results based upon both.

To implement the first approach, the income elasticity of total expenditure on the four main social programmes will be assumed to be equal to one over the period 1981-90; in other words, deflated social expenditure would on average be growing at the same rate as real GDP, and so the share of social expenditure in GDP in nominal terms in 1990 would be the same as in 1981. The assumption that the income elasticity of social expenditure will be one should be compared with past experience. No OECD country listed in Table 2 had so low an elasticity over the period 1960-75. A few countries, however, had elasticities of one or below over the more recent period 1975-81. For a significant number of countries the imposition of so low an elasticity is to demand more than they can be reasonably expected to achieve. But, in some of those countries where the elasticity has been above one, announced budgetary policy suggests a reduction to one or below, and the imposition of an elasticity of one may be offering more leeway than some Member governments themselves intend to permit.

Table 7 shows a decomposition of the future growth rate of social expenditure for the seven major OECD economies, broadly analogous to that which Table 5 provides for the past.

This reports the projected change in the purchasing power of cash benefits relative to general inflation, which is part of the detail of the economic scenario; this is in general very small. Changes in the relative price of education and health services have to be set by assumption; it is assumed that over the period 1981-90 these are held at the rates experienced over the period 1975-81[4]. Population trends up to 1990 have already been charted by the Secretariat[5], and the increase in the number of unemployed between 1981 and 1990 is also embodied in the economic scenario. It will be assumed that the coverage rate for each social programme remains at its 1981 level[6]. Thus, given the growth rate of real GDP, the growth rate of average real benefit across the four major programmes taken together can be estimated[7]. In order to complete the table it is also assumed that average real benefit under each programme – that is education benefits per student, health benefits per person and the purchasing power of social security benefits per recipient – increases at the same rate.

The implied rate of increase in average real benefits is 0.7 per cent per annum. This is less than the growth rate of real GDP (2.1 per cent per annum) because of slightly adverse demographic changes, an increase in the number of old people being largely offset by a fall in the number of young people (see Chart 6), a further increase in the relative price of education and health services, and a small increase in the private consumption deflator relative to the GDP deflator. It is also less than the growth rate of real GDP per capita, which averages 1.8 per cent per annum.

It must be emphasized that the picture presented in Table 7 is based upon numbers which are broad averages, not only across countries but also across social programmes. Thus when it is projected that average real benefits can only increase at 0.7 per cent if the share of social expenditure in GDP in 1990 is not to exceed its 1981 level this is only what is required across the four major programmes taken together. This need not be the rate of increase for each individual programme, although such a pattern has been imposed for computational convenience in preparing Table 7. Average real benefit under some programmes could be allowed to increase faster than this, but then average real benefit under the remainder must inevitably be required to increase more slowly or even decrease.

The differences between the seven major OECD countries can be seen from Table 8, which again refers only to the four main social programmes. A table similar to this for the smaller countries covered in Annex A can be found in Annex B. In none of the seven major OECD countries can the growth rate of average real benefits match the growth rate of real GDP per capita. In Canada and Italy average real benefits have to *fall* at 0.3 and 0.9 per cent per annum respectively, a result of demographic pressures in the first case and relatively poor economic performance combined with a large increase in the relative price of education and health services in the second.

In the preceding analysis the effect on the growth of average real benefits of fixing the share of social expenditure in GDP at its 1981 level has been analysed. The analysis could have proceeded in the opposite direction, making some assumption about the growth rate of average real benefits and deriving the final social expenditure share necessary to support it. The framework used above is sufficiently flexible to accommodate a wide range of approaches and different assumptions. To implement the alternative approach, two separate assumptions will be made about the future growth of welfare services and social security benefits. The first is that average real benefit under each programme will not increase between 1981 and 1990; since the overall impact of demographic change is fairly small this is more or less equivalent to assuming that the real income elasticity of social expenditure is held at zero – i.e. the overall level of service is the same at the end of the period as at the beginning. Looking at Table 4 it is clear that this assumption also is a significant departure from recent experience. To illustrate

47

Table 7. The decomposition of the future growth rate of social expenditure 1981-1990

Average for the seven major OECD countries

	Initial expenditure share	Nominal expenditure	GDP deflator	Deflated expenditure	Relative prices[b]	Real expenditure	Of which: Demography[b]	Of which: Coverage[b]	Of which: Average real benefit	Final expenditure share
	1981	Annual growth rates (%): 1981-1990[a]								1990
Education	5.7	6.7	5.4	1.2	1.3	-0.1	-0.8	0.0	0.7	5.3
Health	5.5	7.5	5.4	2.1	1.0	1.0	0.3	0.0	0.7	5.4
Pensions	8.8	8.0	5.4	2.4	0.3	2.1	1.4	0.0	0.7	9.0
Unemployment compensation	1.2	10.6	5.4	4.9	0.3	4.6	3.9	0.0	0.7	1.5
Total of above programmes	21.2	7.6	5.4	2.1	0.7	1.4	0.7	0.0	0.7	21.2

a) Average compound growth rates, calculated as the geometric mean of the individual country growth rates.
b) See the main text for details of assumptions made in deriving these growth rates.
Source: Secretariat estimates.

Table 8. The decomposition of the future growth rate of social expenditure in the seven major OECD countries 1981-1990

	Initial expenditure share	Nominal expenditure	GDP deflator	Deflated expenditure	Relative prices[b]	Real expenditure	Of which: Demography[b]	Of which: Coverage[b]	Of which: Average real benefit	Final expenditure share
	1981	Annual growth rates (%): 1981-1990[a]								1990
Canada	18.7	7.6	5.5	2.0	0.7	1.3	1.6	0.0	-0.3	18.7
France	26.0	8.6	7.0	1.5	-0.1	1.6	0.3	0.0	1.4	26.0
Germany	25.6	4.6	3.0	1.5	0.6	0.9	-0.3	0.0	1.2	25.6
Italy	26.3	11.7	10.0	1.5	2.0	-0.5	0.4	0.0	-0.9	26.3
Japan	14.9	5.1	1.5	3.5	0.7	2.8	1.3	0.0	1.5	14.9
United Kingdom	20.0	8.1	6.0	2.0	0.1	1.9	0.2	0.0	1.7	20.0
United States	17.6	7.6	5.0	2.5	1.0	1.5	1.2	0.0	0.3	17.6

a) Average compound growth rates.
b) See the main text for details of assumptions made in deriving these growth rates.
Source: Secretariat estimates.

the difference this departure makes, the second assumption is that average real benefit under each programme grows at exactly the same rate as over the period 1975-81.

The impact of these alternative assumptions is summarised in Table 9. A similar table for the smaller OECD countries is included in Annex B. The growth rates of average real benefits consistent with fixed expenditure shares are in general small, so that when no growth in average real benefit is imposed the resulting changes in the share of social expenditure in GDP are also in general small. Any attempt significantly to reduce the social expenditure share would require a reduction in average real benefits: for example, average real benefits would be required to decline at around 2½ per cent per annum on average if the social expenditure share were to be reduced by 25 per cent by 1990. The above "rule-of-thumb" operates in the opposite direction, so that if average real benefits increased at 2.6 per cent, as they did on average between 1975 and 1981, the social expenditure share in 1990 would be about 5 percentage points higher than if average real benefits had not grown at all. Because the country variation in growth rates of average real benefits over the period 1975-81 was large, the consequences for final expenditure shares of allowing growth to continue at these rates vary significantly between countries. If the 1975-81 trend were to continue through to the end of the decade, the expenditure share (in terms of the four major programmes only) in 1990 would be over 30 per cent in France and over 40 per cent in Italy. For the other countries shown in Table 10 the consequences of a continuation of past trends would be a much more modest increase in the expenditure share, and in the case of the United Kingdom the share would fall slightly. Of course, more recent years may have seen some further reductions in the growth rates of average real benefits, implying that this third policy assumption is probably unrealistic. But it reflects the consequences of an attempt to continue making the benefit gains made in a period dominated by economic troubles. With the continuation of slow growth, and even slightly slower growth than previously, it is not a scenario without interest or relevance.

The general conclusion reached above is the following:

- If, as the result of a policy decision, the share of social expenditure in GDP is fixed at its 1981 level;
- If the relative prices of education and health services increase at the same rate as in the recent past;
- If demographic developments are as predicted;
- And if no attempt is made to expand the coverage of existing programmes;

Then it should be possible for average real benefits to increase slightly between 1981 and 1990, although not as fast as real GDP per capita.

This prognosis appears to be relatively comforting. Despite some adverse demographic changes and relative price movements, those gains in programme coverage and levels of benefit made during the 1960s and 1970s need not be conceded. On the contrary, there could be scope for further small gains. The essential features of the Welfare State can be preserved through to 1990.

Naturally, this conclusion has its limitations, although these might not be as restrictive as they initially appear. Obviously the conclusion will reflect any shortcomings in the analysis from which it is derived, and concern is most likely to be expressed about the economic scenario. But this will tend to be regarded as too pessimistic rather than too optimistic, and it is unjustifiable optimism that could undermine the conclusion. However, it may nevertheless be worth investigating how sensitive the conclusion is to the economic scenario on which it is based. To illustrate the likely sensitivity, in Table 10 it is assumed that the growth rate of real GDP is one percentage point higher than in the economic scenario used above in each of the

Table 9. **The relationship between the growth rate of average real benefits and the share of social expenditure in GDP**
1981-1990

| | Initial expenditure share (%) 1981 | Fixed expenditure share | | Policy Assumption | | | | |
| | | | | No growth in average real benefits | | Growth in average real benefits based on the 1975-1981 trend | | |
		Growth rate of average real benefits (%)	Final expenditure share (%) 1990	Growth rate of average real benefits (%)	Final expenditure share (%) 1990	Growth rate of average real benefits (%)	Final expenditure share (%) 1990
Canada	18.7	-0.3	18.7	0.0	19.2	1.3	21.7
France	26.0	1.4	26.0	0.0	23.2	4.1	33.2
Germany	25.6	1.2	25.6	0.0	23.0	1.2	25.6
Italy	26.3	-0.9	26.3	0.0	28.5	4.7	43.0
Japan	14.9	1.5	14.9	0.0	13.1	4.0	18.6
United Kingdom	20.0	1.7	20.0	0.0	17.2	0.7	18.3
United States	17.6	0.3	17.6	0.0	17.1	1.3	19.2
Average	21.2	0.7	21.2	0.0	19.9	2.6	25.0

Sources: Tables 5, 6a-6g, 7 and 8.

Table 10. **The impact of more optimistic economic developments**
1981-1990
Average for the seven major OECD countries

| | Initial expenditure share 1981 | Annual growth rates (%): 1981-1990[a] | | | | | Of which: | | | Final expenditure share 1990 |
		Nominal expenditure	GDP deflator	Deflated expenditure	Relative prices	Real expenditure	Demography	Coverage	Average real benefit	
Education	5.7	7.9	5.4	2.4	1.3	1.1	-0.8	0.0	1.9	5.4
Health	5.5	8.8	5.4	3.2	1.0	2.2	0.3	0.0	1.9	5.5
Pensions	8.8	9.2	5.4	3.6	0.3	3.3	1.4	0.0	1.9	9.2
Unemployment compensation	1.2	7.7	5.4	2.2	0.3	1.9	-0.4	0.0	1.9	1.1
Total of above programmes	21.2	8.7	5.4	3.1	0.7	2.4	0.5	0.0	1.9	21.2

a) Average compound growth rates, calculated as the geometric mean of the individual country growth rates.
Source: Table 7.

seven major OECD countries and that unemployment is held at its 1981 level in all countries except the United States, where it falls steadily. All other elements of the economic scenario remain unchanged, and the growth rate of average real benefits consistent with a fixed expenditure share is calculated as in Table 7.

These more optimistic economic developments would be capable of supporting faster growth in education and health services, and faster growing living standards for the retired, unemployed and other social security benefit recipients. The implied growth rate of these benefits could be of the order of 1.9 per cent per annum rather than 0.7 per cent. The difference between these is a little larger than the 1 percentage point increase in the growth of real GDP because of reduced levels of unemployment. However, the main conclusion above is couched in relative terms, and because the growth rate of real GDP per capita rises from 1.8 to 2.8 per cent, this conclusion remains only slightly affected by a small increase in the assumed rate of growth of real GDP. But the impact is somewhat greater in those countries where unemployment is projected to increase more rapidly, and/or the unemployment compensation programme is relatively large in expenditure terms.

The conclusion also reflects the picture for the typical large country. But the diversity of experience which was a feature of the past is much reduced in the projected future, reflecting convergence of demographic, social and economic developments. In consequence, the above prognosis applies with slightly more or less force to most of the major OECD countries and many of the smaller ones. It must also be remembered that only the medium-term future has been considered. In the longer-term, demographic developments are projected to put more pressure on social expenditure – particularly on the health and pension programmes – as there is likely to be a marked acceleration in the population ageing process throughout the OECD area. Economic developments could also significantly affect the ability to adapt to this pressure. It would therefore be misleading if the principal conclusion of this analysis were used as the basis for any inference about the long-term relationship between economic developments and social expenditure growth.

The conclusion must also be qualified. Even on the basis of the assumptions underlying this analysis, any feeling that satisfying the medium-term budgetary constraint might be

Table 11. **General government deficits**
1975-1983

	Average for the seven major OECD countries[a]		OECD average[a,b]	
	Deficit[c] (As percentage of GDP)	Structural deficit[c] (As percentage of potential GDP)	Deficit[c] (As percentage of GDP)	Structural deficit[c] (As percentage of potential GDP)
1975	4.8	3.2	3.0	1.6
1976	3.6	2.6	2.2	1.4
1977	3.1	2.2	2.1	0.9
1978	3.8	3.3	3.1	1.9
1979	3.2	3.0	3.1	2.5
1980	3.2	2.4	3.1	2.3
1981	4.6	2.2	4.3	2.2
1982	4.8	2.0	5.1	2.5
1983	4.9	1.8	5.1	2.4

a) Unweighted averages.
b) Average for the seven major OECD countries plus Australia, Austria, Belgium, Denmark, Finland, Ireland, Netherlands, Norway and Sweden.
c) Figures for Italy, the United Kingdom and the United States are on a domestic national income account basis and not an SNA basis.
Source: P. Muller and R.W.R. Price, *Structural Budget Deficits and Fiscal Stance*, OECD Economics and Statistics Departement Working Paper 15, OECD, Paris, 1984.

effortless needs to be dispelled. An income elasticity of social expenditure of one may be an ambitious target for some countries to aim at over the period 1981-90. Part of this period is already history. To the extent that some countries overshot social expenditure growth rates consistent with the imposed budgetary stance in 1982 and 1983, some additional restraint will be needed to reach the 1990 target. Equally, recent social expenditure growth rates below those consistent with a fixed expenditure share will provide other countries with the chance to adopt a more relaxed attitude in the future.

This qualification aside, the conclusion that there is no immediate need to begin winding down the major social programmes must remain hedged. Some uncertainty is associated with both the restriction placed on the future scope of the major social programmes and the budgetary policy stance which has been adopted. The first of these uncertainties, which concerns the possibility that present social commitments, fulfilling current expectations and new demands made of social programmes, will require some increase in social expenditure relative to GDP, is discussed in Chapter 4. The second of these uncertainties, intimated already and related to the first, concerns the possibility that the assumption of a fixed share of social expenditure in GDP may be inconsistent with medium-term budgetary policy in a number of countries. In response to government deficits of abnormal and undesirable magnitude, in many countries the burden of economic adjustment is in the process of being shifted from the revenue side to the expenditure side of government accounts.

The medium-term budgetary objective of the majority of OECD countries has been to reduce and stabilize the ratio of the government deficit to GDP through expenditure restraint. The burden of restraint has tended to fall on social programmes. Of course, the growth of expenditure on these programmes helps to explain increasing government deficits. In part, this is a result of the high income elasticity of demand associated with social programmes, adverse demographic trends and problems of expenditure control in the welfare services. But, the principal source of worsening government deficits has been the growth in expenditure and the tax revenue losses associated with increasing unemployment.

Broadly speaking, government deficits can be split into two components, structural and cyclical. The structural component reflects factors related to planning and control mechanisms in the public sector, to the direct impact of inflation on expenditure and taxation, and to the cost of debt servicing, while the cyclical component reflects the reaction of built-in stabilizers to changes in the level of unemployment. It is possible to estimate the cyclical component of budget deficits. The built-in stabilizers are marginal tax rates (including social security contributions) and unemployment benefit, and the cyclical component of the deficit is the net revenue gain in moving from the current growth rate of GDP to a potential growth rate consistent with full employment[8]. Table 11 provides estimates of the cyclically-adjusted or structural deficit yielded by this procedure, expressed as a percentage of potential GDP.

The cyclical component of budget deficits has been significant throughout the period since 1975, and has become particularly important since 1981, as unemployment has grown rapidly. At the same time, discretionary policy initiatives have produced a decrease in structural deficits. Indeed, the United Kingdom has been in structural surplus since 1981 and Germany has more recently moved into surplus. Setting aside expenditure on unemployment compensation, it is the reduction in the structural component of government deficits and the recent moderation in the expenditure growth which are closely linked. If the major social programmes are to find any additional room for expansion in the future, this trend may need to be relaxed, and in some countries even reversed.

NOTES AND REFERENCES

1. OECD *Economic Outlook* 34, December 1983.

2. The projection has been based upon work by the Economics and Statistics Department.

3. This scenario is not inconsistent with the most recent short-term forecast, which is contained in OECD *Economic Outlook* 35, July 1984.

4. It is, of course, difficult to speculate about future productivity changes. But the measured relative price effect is affected by the growth of wages and salaries in the public sector relative to the private sector. The experience of the early 1980s suggests that governments are capable of holding down public sector pay relative to private sector pay, and the assumption made about future changes in the relative prices of education and health services may be too pessimistic.

5. See *Demographic Trends:* 1950-1990, OECD, Paris, 1979.

6. This may be a rather uneasy assumption in the case of unemployment compensation since coverage tends to reflect the stucture of unemployment (the proportion of youths, married women and long-term unemployed) which is itself a function of the level of unemployment, and for the purposes of this exercise the level of unemployment is a demographic variable. Thus what happens to "coverage" may depend upon what is assumed to happen to "demography".

7. Given the annual growth rate of deflated expenditure, which is set equal to the annual growth rate of real GDP to guarantee a fixed expenditure share, weighted averages of the annual growth rates of *relative prices* and *demography* appropriate to each of the four major programmes are taken. The weights are the initial programme shares. Given that *coverage* is assumed constant, an estimate of the growth rate of average real benefit across the four programmes taken together then follows.

8. For a more detailed description of the components of government deficits and the estimation of cyclically-adjusted deficits see Public Sector Deficits: Problems and Policy Implications, OECD *Economic Outlook Occasional Studies,* June 1983.

Chapter 4

SOCIAL EXPENDITURE AND SOCIAL POLICY

OECD countries face similar problems of macro-economic control and adjustment, and these probably leave little or no room for increasing the scope and generosity of the Welfare State over the remainder of the 1980s. In a few countries some further contraction is called for, over and above that which has already taken place in a number of countries. But if there are demands for additional expenditure on certain social programmes, whether those embodied in current practices or those which reflect emerging needs, either the share of social expenditure in GDP must increase, or funds must be directed from lower to higher priority programmes. Only the second of these possibilities is likely to be thought consistent with current macro-economic objectives.

It is not the purpose of this chapter to provide a dispassionate examination of spending priorities in OECD countries. These are inextricably linked with political considerations and the allocation of resources within the Welfare State is unlikely to reflect an assessment of the full range of social needs and the opportunity cost of meeting each. The task of unravelling the complex array of motives which explain existing patterns of expenditure, and constructing a framework for deciding upon the pattern to be aimed for, is probably beyond the scope of this or any single report. But, the importance of establishing a basis for the making of such a decision cannot be over-emphasised. The need or desire to control the growth of social expenditure will pose conflicts and dilemmas, and means of resolving these are a pre-requisite to achieving effective control.

Rather than examine spending priorities, this chapter reflects upon the potential which exists within the Welfare State for the structural adjustment which will inevitably be required if it is to maintain levels of service but spend less, or extend its scope without spending correspondingly more. Thus the focus of attention will be the effectiveness and efficiency of the major social programmes. Rather than an exhaustive investigation of the performance of each programme, it provides a a brief commentary on what appear to be the principal facts and conjectures, many of which are drawn from evidence collected for other studies on social policy to be published by the Secretariat in the near future. A few preliminary observations are offered on the nature of some new demands on social programmes which might exacerbate the problem of controlling social expenditure growth.

1. THE SOURCES OF NEW DEMAND: CURRENT PRACTICES AND EMERGING NEEDS

It would be quite unrealistic to imagine that there will not be increasing demands made of the Welfare State in the 1980s. Existing programmes embody commitments which imply that expenditure will increase over time. For example, pension programmes often only pay a full pension to those who have been contributing to a scheme for the best part of their working life. It will still be many years before some of these programmes reach full maturity, and pension expenditure will rise in the interim. In education and health, where rights of access have been universalized but where utilisation rates in some programmes have been below their potential level, there may also be pressure on expenditure. And where there is no binding commitment, the way people have been treated in the past may set up expectations about the way they and others believe they will be treated in the future. If the increases in average real benefit which this report suggests are feasible conflict with the expectations of those who anticipate levels of service in education and health and the real value of social security benefits increasing at recent rates, governments may be under pressure to increase benefits faster than they would otherwise plan. Opinion surveys and the public statements of opinion leaders suggest that this trend expectation might be an extreme case. But, it seems likely that the demand will be for more expenditure rather than less.

Just as the range of challenges facing the Welfare State was greater in the 1970s than in the 1960s – new needs emerged but few old ones disappeared – so it should be expected that the range of needs will be extended during the 1980s. It is difficult to identify when and where all of these are likely to arise. By their very nature many are largely unpredictable. But it is fairly easy to see whence some will come. The most visible and widely discussed emerging needs in OECD countries are associated with persistent and aggravating labour market difficulties, and in particular the high incidence of unemployment among the young and the growing number of long-term unemployed. The emerging need is not only for additional expenditure on unemployment compensation programmes but also for a systematic approach to the integration of income support and education policies with appropriate employment policies. The urgent requirement is a more flexible labour market which can respond to the new and changing requirements of high technology, to shifting international trade patterns and to increasingly sophisticated consumer tastes through the provision of appropriate training and retraining, selective interventions where necessary to promote labour market adjustment, and the guarantee of adequate support systems for those who, either temporarily or permanently, are not in work. It is important that the adjustment costs of adapting to lower rates of economic growth and higher unemployment be distributed more widely among the workforce and society in general[1].

Extrapolating from recent experience, other sources of future pressure on social expenditure might reflect (in no particular order and not applying with equal force in all countries) the call for more widespread availability of pre-primary education and childcare facilities as the labour force participation of women continues to increase; further advances in medical technology; the desire of welfare consumers for a wider variety of welfare delivery systems; the growing incidence of marital breakdown and the resulting increase in the number of single-parent families; the continuing political thrust for equality of treatment as between men and women under social security provisions; and the need to make preparatory steps in the directions necessary to accommodate ageing populations. On top of this will come any surprises – new demands – the nature, timing and strength of which few can predict.

The inescapable implication of these observations on the possible sources of the new demands on social expenditure is that, as in the 1960s and 1970s, social programmes can expect to face new challenges in the 1980s which are unlikely to be automatically offset elsewhere within the Welfare State. It follows that the problem of controlling the growth of social expenditure is likely to be more difficult than suggested by the straight macro-economic perspective. How much more difficult is impossible to gauge, given the uncertainty associated not only with each potential new demand but also with the nature of the macro-economic constraint. Thus some reference will be made to the flexibility of existing social programmes – their ability to adjust in response to a range of social, demographic and economic pressures – as well as their current effectiveness and efficiency.

2. THE EFFECTIVENESS AND EFFICIENCY OF SOCIAL EXPENDITURE

A. Welfare Objectives

The effectiveness of social expenditure can only be judged in the light of the objectives of the programmes it finances. Social expenditure is normally justified by reference to the revealed inability of the free market to guarantee outcomes which meet society's welfare objectives. These objectives are concerned with the provision of a market in insurance for "social risks", and availability of adequate income support for the needy, and wider equity considerations, including the provision of merit goods and income redistribution.

Everybody at some time runs the risk of getting sick or injured, becoming disabled, widowed, or unemployed, or requiring financial support during old-age for longer than anticipated. These are not risks fully serviced by the private insurance market, which either rejects the opportunity to provide insurance or supplies insurance which is judged inadequate. The failure of the private market is predictable. A private insurer is not going to provide insurance against sickness or unemployment when he is incapable of judging its cause (the moral hazard problem); he will provide health, injury and permanent health insurance, but only at a price determined by the distribution of bad risks and for a predetermined indemnity (the adverse selection problem); he will finance unanticipated longevity, but since he cannot usually secure a guaranteed real return on his investments he is not in a position to specify the real income he will pay to the retired (capital market failure). There is a clear role for government if these social risks are to be adequately insured. This could involve intervention in the private market, although more commonly the State bears these risks itself.

Even if social insurance were freely available, it seems unlikely that these risks would be adequately insured in the sense that everybody purchased some minimum amount of cover; some would reject this opportunity by choice, while insurance might be beyond the means of others. Thus being out of the workforce or out of employment would be associated with widespread financial hardship and poverty. Moreover, even some people in work would find their earnings insufficient to support dependants, either in normal circumstances or where an unusually large financial commitment is required (for example, when a disabled dependant has to be cared for). It is a widely accepted responsibility of the State to try to guarantee that living standards do not fall below some socially acceptable minimum level.

Society's equity objectives typically extend beyond those implied by the provision of social insurance and income support. In a private education market, the children of the rich are most likely to be taught by the most accomplished teachers in the best equipped schools, and society's equity objective in education is therefore to promote equality of educational opportunity. In a private health market, the best health care would be received by those most able to pay, and the poor might not be able to afford health care at all. Here society's equity objective is to provide equality of access to adequate health care for those with equal need. The tendency is to view education and health as merit goods, which people would choose to consume in insufficient quantity even at a subsidised price and where governments prefer to exercise control over quality, and this is why governments usually provide these services themselves rather than intervene in the private market.

Income, wealth and social welfare are unequally distributed in all OECD countries, and redistribution is an objective of society and the State. Certainly, income support policies imply redistribution, but governments have at their disposal a much wider range of instruments with which to achieve redistributive goals. Taxation, the method of financing social insurance and income support programmes, and legislation relating to employment and pay all affect the distribution of income. But net income – income after all taxes and social security contributions have been paid and all cash benefits received – is too narrow a concept of income on which to base conclusions about the distribution of social welfare. Benefits in kind – health care and education received being the prime examples – are a major contribution to the well-being of those who receive them. When their monetary equivalent is added to net income, the distribution of the final income measure so produced should provide a better guide to the overall distribution of social welfare[2]. Redistribution is also regarded as providing external benefits to those who are not themselves in need. There is a certain pleasure to be gained from living in a society where others are reasonably well educated, healthy and protected from destitution.

There is a well established role for the Welfare State which is firmly rooted in the idea of market failure and the desire for distributional justice. But equally the State has a responsibility to society which supports its activities to pursue their shared objectives responsibly. Not only does this require careful monitoring of the success with which objectives are being met, but also continuous assessment of the efficiency of the mechanisms set up to implement the policies designed to meet these objectives. Society and the State have largely failed to evaluate their social welfare policies thoroughly in decades past.

B. Education and Health

While neither equality of educational opportunity nor equality of educational outcome are well defined, government intervention has resulted in higher educational standards and has been responsible for some improvement in social mobility and the distribution of earnings through its influence on education standards. Government intervention has improved access to health care and thereby both a higher general level of health and more equal health standards have resulted. In these senses, and in terms of their indirect beneficial effects on the economy, intervention in education and health has been successful. But, doubt has been expressed whether current levels of State involvement achieve very much more success than involvement on a far more modest scale could secure, although the evidence is mixed. Certainly, in some countries, increasing education and health expenditure in the late 1960s and 1970s has not been accompanied by the equity gains made in earlier years – as reflected in, for example, increased social mobility, a more equal distribution of earnings, or lower morbidity and mortality rates – and some earlier gains may have since been eroded. But in other countries notable progress has been made, particularly in the case of health care, and even in those countries where there appears to have been been little overall progress the evidence is that major gains have been made by some disadvantaged groups in society.

Furthermore, underlying inequalities in the distribution of income, wealth and power seem to place limits on the redistribution which can be achieved through expenditure on education and health. Because State provision aims to achieve, among other things, equality of opportunity in education and equality of access to health care, the monetary equivalent of the benefit provided by these services is greatest for those who can best exploit the freedoms entailed in respect of services where a large element of choice can be exercised. This tends to be the better informed, more articulate and highly motivated middle classes. This applies far more so in the case of education than health, and particularly to upper secondary and higher education. In the case of health care the problem is one of low take-up of benefits by low income people in need. Underlying inequalities have thus proved fairly resistant to change. The economic and social barriers which prevent poorer members of the community from taking full advantage of the options open to them have proved difficult to break down. On equity grounds the success of government intervention in education and (probably much less so) in health, while not inconsiderable, has probably been over-rated. Moreover, the cost of even incomplete success is reflected not only in the public expenditure devoted to these programmes, but also in the consequences of intervention for the efficiency with which education and health care are provided, and for their flexibility of response to the changing environment in which they are required to operate.

There are three principal and related sources of inefficiency in the provision of education and health services. First, these services are in general collectively provided and supplied free or at only a notional price to individuals, and thus benefits are necessarily divorced from costs. This has generated unnecessary demand for certain types of service and has resulted in a misallocation of resources between different kinds of service. Second, and a consequence of the first, governments have had little choice but to allocate resources to the provision of education and health on the basis of mainly non-budgetary criteria. And third, a consequence of the previous two and also a function of the difficulty the consumer has in judging the quality of education and health care provision, the services are dominated by well-organised supplying professionals. Thus teachers have been free to devise curricula often overly concentrated on specialized formal and academic education at the expense of the development of more general pre-vocational skills, and to emphasise the teaching function at the expense of the learning process. In the case of health care natural incentives, the frequent absence of adequate cost-effectiveness criteria and an understandable desire to operate where possible at the frontier of medical technology have combined to persuade doctors and other medical practitioners to offer a maximum rather than an optimum response to patients' demands.

The professionalisation of these services has not only been a principal contributory factor in the increase in education and health expenditure, but has also created rigidities in supply. Education and health professionals have grown accustomed to the discretion that current structures have conferred upon them. Any attempt to introduce more appropriate types of educational courses into schools, colleges and universities, or to involve patients more fully in medical decisions – and the related call for further health education and preventive health care this probably entails – is likely to be viewed as a move to dispossess these professionals of some of their freedom and therefore meets with resistance. Thus any attempts to protect the current range of services in the face of economic pressures, or to extend or trade-off services in response to new demands, are hampered by insufficient flexibility.

C. Social Security

In terms of the objectives of insurance, income support and redistribution set out above, social security systems are a success. A wide range of insurance benefits is provided, and where private market alternatives are available they fail in many respects to match the quality attained by public arrangements. If it were not for extensive income support programmes, the number of people in poverty and the degree of the hardship suffered by the poor would be much greater. Moreover, social security benefits are the major force behind reductions in income inequality in OECD countries[3]. But these successes can disguise weaknesses, the most serious of which is the coincidence of social insurance programmes which pay generous earnings-related benefits to some people with income support programmes which leave others with low incomes and in poverty.

Adequate earnings-related benefits for the sick, unemployed, retired and others are paid only to those who were reasonably paid when in work. Their rationale follows directly from the insurance characteristic of these programmes, but it is a rationale which becomes subject to severe strains when, as at present, unemployment is widespread and unevenly distributed and when those in work have little discretionary income which they are willing to devote to further insurance. On a private insurance market the better-off would presumably choose to buy more insurance, and this feature is built into the substitute State arrangements. Naturally, the low paid tend to receive only small social insurance benefits, sometimes not sufficiently large to keep them out of poverty, and therefore have to rely on these being topped-up with income-tested benefits, the failings of which – principally that they are not paid automatically and have to be claimed and that they sometimes combine with income tax to produce very high marginal tax rates for the low paid – partly explain the persistence of poverty. While the fact that they have failed to eliminate poverty is their most serious failing, social security arrangements have other weaknesses. There is a possibility that the amount of insurance people are forced to buy is excessive, both from the individual and the collective point of view. And the relatively unfavourable treatment of certain groups of beneficiaries, without any apparent rationale, and the wide range of distortions to the choice between work and leisure they often imply, are also regularly cited as shortcomings.

The persistence of income poverty may seem surprising, since in aggregate the minimum amount of money which still needs to be transferred directly to the poor to totally eliminate poverty is in many countries relatively small. Moreover, it tends to be much less than the sum of money currently paid to those who would not otherwise be poor, or the sum paid in total to each otherwise poor person over and above that needed to eliminate their poverty. But it does not follow that the poverty which remains can be eliminated at only modest cost.

Inefficiency in social security tends to arise as a result of the way in which benefit entitlement is established. The important distinctions are between benefits which are income-tested and those which are contingent upon status – i.e. being retired or unemployed, and between flat-rate and earnings-related benefits. Income tested benefits are efficient in the sense that they are not paid to those who do not need them. Contingent benefits, in that they are paid without any reference to recipients' current income, can be inefficient. However, if the contingent benefit is flat-rate the inefficiency is typically not large, simply because being retired, unemployed, or a member of any other contingent group carries with it a high probability of being poor in the absence of social security.

Most countries rely upon a mixture of these different types of benefit, and the majority of benefit recipients are not poor, at least by official or widely-accepted standards. That poverty remains largely reflects the inadequacy of contingent benefits, and the failure to take-up income-tested benefits. Increasing and extending the scope of contingent benefits is costly, since the incomes of the non-poor majority are necessarily increased. Introducing more targeting or selectivity into the payment of benefits, while at the same time guaranteeing that these are paid to everybody who ought to be receiving them, is also costly, since the incomes of many others may also have to be enhanced.

3.   IMPROVING EFFECTIVENESS AND EFFICIENCY

The successes of the modern Welfare State are considerable; but weaknesses are also apparent. Failings in the areas of education, health and social security have been pointed to. These programmes are less effective than they ought to be since society's equity objectives remain unfulfilled, and there is a suspicion that too high a price is paid for the successes which are achieved. Thus in education and health in particular, if equity gains are secured this must probably be at the price of structural change and the reallocation of resources within the services, and not more expansion. If there is the political will to implement the necessary changes, not only can the quality of these services be improved but also there might be further redistribution, including the alleviation of poverty, as the incidence of low education and health standards, which are associated with inequality and poverty, is reduced. And even if major redistributive gains prove impossible, more equality and the elimination of poverty can still be sought through reform of social security systems.

A. Education and Health

Because the education and health programmes have aims which are strongly redistributive in intent, no matter how great the proven or suspected inefficiencies in the provision of these services may be, the fact that these aims are being met to an extent that could not, or at least would not, be achieved if individuals acted on their own implies that collective provision is unlikely to be wholly rejected in favour of the free market. Equally, the dissatisfaction implied by the criticism which is often levelled at heavy State involvement in education and health care provision gives genuine cause for concern.

Under an institutional structure of this kind the task of improving effectiveness and efficiency resolves itself into a management issue, and in particular the establishment of criteria by which management is judged to be successful. Since the products of the two services have a social dimension, valued in intangible qualitative terms as well as by measurable results, the setting of targets is inevitably difficult, and becomes even more so in a period of financial restraint when one social objective can only be pursued at the expense of another. Given this problem, the central issue revolves around the potential for realising the improvements in effectiveness and efficiency which are sought in some retreat from the current level of State involvement. For example, the State could substantially withdraw from the production process itself. The State would retain the responsibility for providing finance, prudential regulation, and guiding the services towards specific outcomes. But the purely management function would be subjected to the disciplines of the market. Alternatively, the State could limit the open-endedness of present commitments, for example by restricting public liability in respect of certain types of service and by charging for some others. The introduction of a measure of privatisation – broadly defined – into education and health services would probably have to be accompanied by other developments if it is to succeed.

First, any significant move towards privatisation, in either education or health, is likely to render more visible the redistributive aspects of the programmes. General reductions in State support in a particular area may need to be qualified by much more specific targeting policies towards the disadvantaged. Second, policies of privatisation and closer targeting may be most effective if they are associated with policies of decentralisation, again broadly defined. Local participation and scrutiny of education and health services is likely to be more vigorous and open than that of a central monitoring agency, particularly if the local agency is credited with some budgetary power and discretion in resource use. Third, no matter whether the management of education and health services is in private or public hands, the inflexibilities inherent in the existing labour force and professional structures will need to be tackled. Only then might a significant degree of privatisation and decentralisation induce more care and efficiency in the use of resources while maintaining effectiveness. And even if the movement towards these alternative delivery systems – which has already started – fails in this respect, privatisation and decentralisation have their own sources of inspiration and a built-in momentum which may ultimately result in more effective and flexible welfare provisions, although in terms of the resources devoted to these activities not necessarily cheaper ones. This serves to highlight the urgency of continuing the search for the improved management and administration techniques which could be the key to improvements in efficiency.

B. Social Security

The weaknesses associated with social security arrangements could be overcome if benefits were also targeted to a much greater extent than at present. But targeting, not only of social security benefits but also education and health schemes, is synonymous with some form of income-testing, the usual requirement being that a statement of resources must accompany any claim for benefit. For various reasons, income-testing of this sort has proved a deterrent to claiming, people choosing to forgo a benefit rather than volunteer a claim. Only if there were an automatic income test, and the need to claim were abandoned, could this problem be overcome and benefits successfully targeted towards all those in need. In the case of social security benefits, a desire to bring an end to claiming leads naturally to thought of some sort of integrated tax and benefit system.

Many countries have in the past investigated such systems – negative tax schemes, tax credit schemes, social dividend schemes etc. – but problems concerning the appropriate structure of these systems, and in particular the high marginal tax rates they often imply, and their administration, although not insurmountable, have provided a barrier to the implementation of integrated systems. Nevertheless the combination of the high cost, complication and partial failure of existing programmes has awakened some interest in these systems, although this has been largely confined to the possibility of integrating existing income-tested benefits into the tax system rather than any significant extension of targeting.

C. Redistributive Efficiency

It has been noted that the benefits from expenditure on education and health care accrue mainly to the middle classes, and that while social security benefits constitute a large share of the income of those at the bottom of the income distribution they also make a contribution to the incomes of those further up the distribution, and even the fairly well-off. The gross flows of resources implied by the current structure and administration of social programmes far exceed the net flows which ultimately result[4]. In principle, the same amount of redistribution which results could be achieved with vastly reduced gross flows; indeed, post-war increases in social expenditure have been accompanied by little discernible reduction in social and economic inequality. The redistributive inefficiency which results from this churning or circularity in resource flows has in itself been a source of concern about current levels of social expenditure. The related questions of economic inefficiency resulting from tax-and-benefit induced distortions associated with large social programmes and their heavy revenue requirements – the reduced incentives to work, save and take risks – and any behavioural responses they imply, along with the resulting prejudicial influence on the private provision of social goods, have served to heighten this concern.

The large excess of gross flows over net flows is the logical consequence of the widespread reliance on social programmes the programmes themselves have encouraged, and while it might appear that gains in redistributive efficiency are there for the taking, this dependence on social programmes throughout the range of incomes makes the reality somewhat different. While society has redistributive objectives, not each and every programme should be required to redistribute income in accordance with these objectives. Success in meeting society's

61

redistributive objectives should be judged by reference to the final outcome which reflects the combined impact of all programmes. To pursue only redistributive objectives on a programme-by-programme basis must mean that other objectives – possibly of equal or greater importance – have to be conceded. There are unlikely to be significant costless or even low-cost gains in redistributive efficiency to be made. But the pressure to seek such gains may be irresistible.

4. REFORMING THE WELFARE STATE

The major source of concern about social expenditure growth has been economic, and has centred on the ability to continue supporting plans formulated in the affluent 1960s and early 1970s. A few years ago a bleak picture was painted, and the need to make unpalatable decisions as to social priorities seemed the inevitable consequence of economic pressures alone. It now appears that this was a rather pessimistic view, and that to the end of the 1980s existing social programmes can survive more or less unamended, even if there is little scope for improvement. But while the "economic crisis" of the Welfare State may have peaked, it seems likely that the process of major institutional reform has only just begun. There is certainly no room for complacency. The above conclusion only follows from an examination of future social expenditure growth within a narrow accounting framework. Wider economic, political and social pressures on the Welfare State will in all probability call for significant structural adjustment.

The necessary adjustments cannot be decided upon and implemented hastily. The inefficiency and inflexibility of current social programmes have been emphasised. The responses to recent economic crises have resulted in some small improvement in these respects. But the dominant response has been to control welfare spending across-the-board or where resistance was expected to be more diffuse, with little attention being paid to the effect on the effectiveness and efficiency of social expenditure of distributing the impact of spending restraint in different ways between programmes. It is therefore not surprising that much remains to be done before the Welfare State can be said to be in a position where it can adequately respond to the pressures facing it. To endow the system with the necessary efficiency and flexibility, while maintaining effectiveness, requires a careful assessment of needs and costs which has so far been lacking, and some consideration of alternative forms of welfare delivery.

And even once appropriate reforms have been identified, there will be a long lag between implementation and outcome. Reforming the Welfare State has necessarily to be a long-term objective. Many people are dependent on welfare services and social security benefits, and it would be unreasonable both to frustrate their expectations and to expect them to make alternative arrangements at relatively short notice. The aged would be particularly badly affected by hastily implemented reforms. They tend to be largely reliant on State pensions and the State provision of health care. The case for respecting the expectations of other groups is also strong. Even the fairly affluent middle classes who have come to rely on health and education services provided by the State would require time before they could be expected to make the financial provisions which would enable them to pay for these services, whether they are provided by the State or the private sector. And if it is intended that the State's involvement in service provision is to be reduced, it will also take time for the private sector to reach a position from which it can assume this responsibility.

A second reason why it would be difficult to walk away from existing arrangements is that there is an element of *quid pro quo* underlying current financing arrangements, whereby certain groups in society are willing to transfer resources to others on the understanding that they will be similarly treated by others should they seek the support of the Welfare State. The reform of the Welfare State would require agreement about a new financing arrangement and its implementation, a process which can only be successfully concluded – in the sense that the old arrangement has few remaining financial consequences – after a considerable passage of time. To simply abandon the old arrangement and replace it with one that imposes unanticipated costs on a large number of people would not only rob many of what they quite reasonably view as their natural right but might also leave the Welfare State without the shared commitment to a caring society upon which it depends for survival.

This problem takes on particular significance in the case of old-age pensions. Throughout the 1960s and 1970s the population slowly aged in the majority of OECD countries; this ageing process will continue through to the end of the 1980s, and for a long time thereafter. Many countries are expressing concern about the problems of financing old-age pensions with a much older population. This concern has a firm basis, although it has not been revealed in the present analysis. The pension financing problem emerges when the post-war baby-boom generation begins to retire – in around 2010 – and becomes really severe some twenty years later. It is not a problem of the 1980s and 1990s. But, given what has just been said about the process of welfare reform, the solution should perhaps be sought in the 1980s for implementation in the 1990s since it inevitably implies a transition to a more flexible pension contract, with either lower benefits (possibly involving some adjustment of retirement age), higher contributions or some combination of the two.

Clearly, appropriate reform of the Welfare State should neither be decided upon nor introduced in haste. Successful reform demands that social programmes are tailored to both social needs and limited resources. At the same time, an attempt must be made to maintain the economic means to support a broad, flexible but still humanitarian set of social programmes. The carefully planned strategy necessary to achieve what is likely to be a more pluralist system of welfare should involve integrated social and economic policies not necessarily of the same magnitude, but certainly born of the sort of vision, which led to the creation of the modern Welfare State.

NOTES AND REFERENCES

1. The problems involved in promoting labour market flexibility, and some of the strategies which might be adopted, are discussed in *The Challenge of Unemployment: A Report to Labour Ministers*, OECD, Paris, 1982.

2. But it obviously remains imperfect. Wealth confers considerable power over resources which the income flow it yields only partly reflects. And, as pointed out in Chapter 2, income itself is in some cases a poor guide to standard of living. There are also problems in making inferences about social welfare from information on the equivalent monetary value of education and, particularly, health services consumed.

3. Evidence on the impact of social security on income levels and income distribution can be found in *Public Expenditure on Income Maintenance Programmes*, OECD Studies in Resource Allocation, OECD, Paris, 1976 and M. Sawyer, *Income Distribution in OECD Countries*, OECD Occasional Study, OECD, Paris, 1976.

4. There are numerous country studies which reveal the excess of gross flows over net flows. These are reviewed in P. Saunders, *Evidence on Income Redistribution by Governments*, OECD Economics and Statistics Department Working Paper No. 11, OECD, Paris, 1984.

Annex A

THE DECOMPOSITION OF THE GROWTH RATE OF SOCIAL EXPENDITURE IN SMALLER OECD COUNTRIES

Table A1. **The decomposition of the growth rate of social expenditure in smaller OECD countries**
1960-1975 and 1975-1981

Australia

	Initial expenditure share	Nominal expenditure	GDP deflator	Deflated expenditure	Relative prices	Real expenditure	Of which:			Final expenditure share
							Demography	Coverage	Average real benefit	
	1960									1975
					Annual growth rates (%): 1960-1975[a]					
Education	2.8	17.3	5.8	10.9	1.8	8.9	2.1	-0.5	7.2	6.1
Health	2.4	17.6	5.8	11.1	-1.8	9.1	2.0	1.8	5.1	5.6
Pensions	3.4	14.3	5.8	8.1	-0.4	8.5	2.2	2.6	3.5	5.0
Unemployment compensation	0.1	31.0	5.8	23.8	-0.4	24.3	10.9	1.1	10.9	0.7
Total of above programmes	8.7	16.4	5.8	10.0	0.9	9.0	2.2	1.4	5.2	17.4
Total social expenditure	10.2	15.9	5.8	9.6	0.9	8.6	-	-	-	18.8
	1975									1981
					Annual growth rates (%): 1975-1981[a]					
Education	6.1	11.6	9.9	1.5	0.3	1.2	0.2[b]	0.2[b]	0.8	5.8
Health	5.6	9.6	9.9	-0.2	0.3	-0.5	1.2	1.3	-2.9	4.7
Pensions	5.0	14.7	9.9	4.3	0.3	4.0	3.1[b]	-0.3[b]	1.2	5.6
Unemployment compensation	0.7	15.5	9.9	5.1	0.3	4.8	5.1	11.8	-10.8	0.8
Total of above programmes	17.4	12.0	9.9	1.9	0.3	1.6	1.6	0.9	-0.8	16.9
Total social expenditure	18.8	12.6	9.9	2.4	0.1	2.3	-	-	-	18.8

a) Average compound growth rates.
b) 1975-1980.
Sources: See Table 5: data on coverage under unemployment compensation schemes from *Yearbook of Australia*.

Table A2. **Finland**

	Initial expenditure share 1960	Nominal expenditure	GDP deflator	Deflated expenditure	Relative prices	Real expenditure	Of which: Demography	Of which: Coverage	Of which: Average real benefit	Final expenditure share 1975
				Annual growth rates (%): 1960-1975[a]						
Education	6.6	13.2	8.2	4.6	1.6	3.0	−0.6	1.0	2.6	6.6
Health	2.3	19.1	8.2	10.1	−1.6	11.9	0.4	0.0	11.5	4.9
Pensions	3.3	19.3	8.2	10.3	−0.8	11.1	2.8	−0.04	8.0	7.3
Unemployment compensation	0.0	41.4	8.2	30.6	−0.8	31.7	3.4	27.6	−0.2	0.2
Total of above programmes	12.2	16.0	8.2	7.2	0.3	6.9	0.4	0.6	4.9	19.0
Total social expenditure	15.4	16.3	8.2	7.5	0.1	7.4	–	–	–	23.3
	1975			*Annual growth rates (%): 1975-1981[a]*						1981
Education	6.6	11.9	9.7	2.0	0.3	1.7	−1.3[b]	0.8[b]	2.2	6.3
Health	4.9	13.8	9.7	3.7	−0.2	3.9	0.3	0.0	3.6	5.2
Pensions	7.3	16.5	9.7	6.2	0.7	5.5	2.5	−0.5	3.4	8.8
Unemployment compensation	0.2	33.0	9.7	21.2	0.6	20.5	16.1	20.4	−14.8	0.6
Total of above programmes	19.0	14.7	9.7	4.3	0.4	3.9	0.8	0.3	2.8	20.9
Total social expenditure	23.3	15.0	9.7	4.8	0.3	4.5	–	–	–	25.9

a) Average compound growth rates.
b) 1975-1980.
Sources: See Table 5; data on coverage under unemployment compensation schemes from *Statistisk Arsbok for Finland*.

67

Table A3. **Ireland**

	Initial expenditure share	Nominal expenditure	GDP deflator	Deflated expenditure	Relative prices	Real expenditure	Of which: Demography	Of which: Coverage	Of which: Average real benefit	Final expenditure share
	1960									1975
				Annual growth rates (%): 1960-1975[a]						
Education	3.0	18.1	8.0	9.3	1.8	7.4	1.3[b]	1.0[b]	5.0	6.1
Health	3.0	18.4	8.0	9.7	1.8	7.7	0.9[c]	7.2[c]	-0.4	6.4
Pensions	2.5	16.6	8.0	7.9	-0.3	8.2	0.7[c]	1.5[c]	5.9	4.3
Unemployment compensation	0.6	23.1	8.0	14.0	-0.3	14.3	1.0	–	–	2.3
Total of above programmes[d]	8.5	17.8	8.0	9.0	1.2	7.7	1.0	3.3	3.4	16.8
Total social expenditure	11.7	17.8	8.0	9.1	0.8	8.2	–	–	–	23.1
	1975									1981
				Annual growth rates (%): 1975-1981[a]						
Education	6.1	21.7	14.6	6.2	1.6	4.5	1.4	-0.2	3.3	7.1
Health	6.4	23.9	14.6	8.1	1.7	6.3	1.4	2.7	2.1	8.4
Pensions	4.3	22.6	14.6	7.0	0.4	6.6	1.1	0.7	4.7	5.2
Unemployment compensation	2.3	20.1	14.6	4.8	0.4	4.4	10.5	-1.6	-4.0	2.5
Total of above programmes	19.1	22.4	14.6	6.8	1.2	5.6	2.4	0.8	2.3	23.2
Total social expenditure	23.1	22.7	14.6	7.1	1.0	6.0	–	–	–	28.4

a) Average compound growth rates.
b) 1965-1975.
c) 1961-1975.
d) Excluding unemployment compensation.
Sources: See Table 5; data on coverage under unemployment compensation schemes from *Statistical Abstract of Ireland*.

68

Table A4. **Netherlands**

| | Initial expenditure share | Nominal expenditure | GDP deflator | Deflated expenditure | Relative prices | Real expenditure | Of which: | | | Final expenditure share |
							Demography	Coverage	Average real benefit	
	1960									1975
				Annual growth rates (%): 1960-1975[a]						
Education	4.5	15.2	6.6	8.1	3.6	4.3	0.7	1.2	2.3	7.6
Health	1.3	23.1	6.6	15.5	3.7	11.4	1.2	1.3	8.7	5.9
Pensions	5.2	16.8	6.6	9.6	-0.6	10.3	2.7	-0.2	7.6	10.7
Unemployment compensation	0.2	19.9	6.6	12.5	-0.6	13.2	13.5	–	–	0.7
Total of above programmes[b]	11.0	16.9	6.6	9.7	1.6	8.0	1.7	0.6	5.6	24.2
Total social expenditure	16.2	17.6	6.6	10.4	1.0	9.3	–	–	–	37.1
	1975									1981
				Annual growth rates (%): 1975-1981[a]						
Education	7.6	6.9	5.9	0.9	-0.2	1.1	-0.5[c]	0.3[c]	1.3	7.1
Health	5.9	10.4	5.9	4.2	-0.2	4.4	0.6	2.5	1.2	6.7
Pensions	10.7	11.7	5.9	5.5	0.3	5.2	2.0[c]	0.4[c]	2.7	13.0
Unemployment compensation	0.7	14.2	5.9	7.8	0.3	7.5	12.0	0.2	-4.2	1.0
Total of above programmes	24.9	10.0	5.9	3.9	0.0	3.8	1.2	0.9	1.7	27.8
Total social expenditure	37.1	7.6	5.9	1.6	0.2	1.4	–	–	–	36.1

a) Average compound growth rates.
b) Excluding unemployment compensation.
c) 1975-1980.
Sources: See Table 5; data on coverage under unemployment compensation schemes from *Sociale Maandstatistiek*.

Table A5. New Zealand

	Initial expenditure share 1960	Nominal expenditure	GDP deflator	Deflated expenditure	Relative prices	Real expenditure	Of which: Demography	Of which: Coverage	Of which: Average real benefit	Final expenditure share 1975
						Annual growth rates (%): 1960-1975[a]				
Education	2.7	13.8	5.6	7.7	2.4	5.2	1.9	-0.5	3.8	4.5
Health	3.3	12.0	5.6	6.0	2.4	3.5	1.8	0.0	1.7	4.4
Pensions	4.4	10.9	5.6	5.0	-0.2	5.2	1.9	0.7	2.5	5.1
Unemployment compensation	0.0	28.4	5.6	21.3	-0.2	21.5	7.6	7.8	4.7	0.1
Total of above programmes	10.4	12.0	5.6	6.0	1.3	4.7	1.9	0.2	2.5	14.1
Total social expenditure	13.0	11.5	5.6	5.5	1.1	4.4	–	–	–	16.3
	1975					Annual growth rates (%): 1975-1981[a]				1981
Education	4.5	16.4	16.1	0.3	1.2	-0.9	-0.8[b]	0.0[b]	-0.1	4.5
Health	4.4	18.5	16.1	2.1	1.2	0.9	0.3	0.0	0.6	4.8
Pensions	5.1	23.8	16.1	6.6	-1.0	7.7	2.5	3.6	1.4	7.3
Unemployment compensation	0.1	62.5	16.1	40.1	-1.0	41.3	59.3	-4.6	-7.0	0.5
Total of above programmes	14.1	20.0	16.1	3.4	0.4	3.1	0.8	1.3	0.6	17.1
Total social expenditure	16.3	20.2	16.1	3.5	-0.2	3.7	–	–	–	19.6

a) Average compound growth rates.
b) 1975-1980.
Sources: See Table 5; data on coverage under unemployment compensation schemes from *New Zealand Official Yearbook*.

Table A6. Norway

	Initial expenditure share 1960	Nominal expenditure	GDP deflator	Deflated expenditure	Relative prices	Real expenditure	Of which: Demography	Of which: Coverage	Of which: Average real benefit	Final expenditure share 1975
		Annual growth rates (%): 1960-1975[a]								
Education	3.8	14.8	5.9	8.3	1.3	6.9	0.7	0.6	5.5	6.7
Health	2.8	17.0	5.9	10.4	1.3	9.0	0.7	0.0	8.2	6.4
Pensions	2.8	18.4	5.9	11.8	-0.3	12.1	2.1	2.8	6.8	7.9
Unemployment compensation	0.2	8.4	5.9	2.3	-0.3	2.6	11.9[b]	-2.7[b]	-5.8	0.1
Total of above programmes	9.6	16.4	5.9	9.8	0.8	8.9	1.3	1.0	6.4	21.1
Total social expenditure	11.7	16.7	5.9	10.1	0.5	9.5	–	–	–	26.2
	1975	Annual growth rates (%): 1975-1981[a]								1981
Education	6.7	12.3	9.6	2.4	-1.2	3.6	-0.5	2.3	1.8	6.1
Health	6.4	14.0	9.6	4.0	-1.2	5.2	0.4	0.0	4.8	6.4
Pensions	7.9	14.0	9.6	4.2	-0.4	4.6	1.9	0.4	2.2	7.9
Unemployment compensation	0.1	31.8	9.6	20.3	-0.4	20.8	0.0	15.2	4.9	0.3
Total of above programmes	21.1	13.5	9.6	3.6	-0.9	4.5	0.7	1.0	2.9	20.7
Total social expenditure	26.2	14.7	9.6	4.6	-0.9	5.6	–	–	–	27.1

a) Average compound growth rates.
b) 1965-1975.
Sources: See Table 5; data on coverage under unemployment compensation schemes from *Statistik Arbok*.

Table A7. **Sweden**

	Initial expenditure share 1960	Nominal expenditure	GDP deflator	Deflated expenditure	Relative prices	Real expenditure	Of which: Demography	Of which: Coverage	Of which: Average real benefit	Final expenditure share 1975
		Annual growth rates (%): 1960-1975[a]								
Education	4.6	11.5	5.8	5.4	1.9	3.4	0.2	1.0	2.2	5.7
Health	3.4	15.6	5.8	9.3	-1.8	11.3	0.6	0.0	10.6	7.2
Pensions	4.4	14.5	5.8	8.3	-0.4	8.7	2.3[b]	0.2[b]	6.0	8.2
Unemployment compensation	0.2	12.7	5.8	6.6	-0.4	7.0	0.4	–	–	0.2
Total of above programmes[c]	12.4	13.7	5.8	7.5	0.1	7.4	1.1	0.4	5.9	21.1
Total social expenditure	15.4	14.1	5.8	7.9	-0.1	8.0	–	–	–	26.9
	1975	Annual growth rates (%): 1975-1981[a]								1981
Education	5.7	14.1	10.2	3.6	1.5	2.1	-0.3	1.7	0.7	6.6
Health	7.2	15.1	10.2	4.5	1.1	3.4	0.3	0.0	3.1	8.9
Pensions	8.2	18.2	10.2	7.2	0.3	6.9	1.7	2.7	2.3	11.8
Unemployment compensation	0.2	26.5	10.2	14.9	0.3	14.5	8.3	–	–	0.5
Total of above programmes[c]	21.1	16.0	10.2	5.3	0.9	4.4	0.7	1.5	2.1	27.3
Total social expenditure	26.9	15.4	10.2	4.7	0.7	4.0	–	–	–	33.4

a) Average compound growth rates.
b) 1963-1975.
c) Excluding unemployment compensation.
Sources: See Table 5.

72

Annex B

THE DECOMPOSITION OF THE FUTURE
GROWTH RATE OF SOCIAL EXPENDITURE AND THE RELATIONSHIP
BETWEEN THE GROWTH RATE OF AVERAGE REAL BENEFITS AND THE
SHARE OF SOCIAL EXPENDITURE IN GDP IN SMALLER OECD COUNTRIES

Table B1. **The decomposition of the future growth rate of social expenditure in smaller OECD countries 1981-1990**

	Initial expenditure share 1981	Nominal expenditure	GDP deflator	Deflated expenditure	Relative prices[b]	Real expenditure	Of which: Demography[b]	Of which: Coverage[b]	Of which: Average real benefit	Final expenditure share 1990
		Annual growth rates (%): 1981-1990[a]								
Australia	16.9	10.2	7.5	2.5	0.5	2.0	1.8	0.0	0.2	16.9
Finland	20.9	11.2	8.0	3.0	0.2	2.8	0.5	0.0	2.3	20.9
Ireland	23.2	12.2	10.0	2.0	1.8	0.2	1.9	0.0	-1.7	23.2
Netherlands	27.8	5.0	4.0	1.0	-0.1	1.1	1.1	0.0	0.0	27.8
New Zealand	17.1	7.5	7.0	0.5	0.9	-0.4	1.1	0.0	-1.5	17.1
Norway	20.7	8.1	6.0	2.0	-0.1	2.1	0.4	0.0	1.7	20.7
Sweden	27.8	9.2	6.5	2.5	0.9	1.6	0.0	0.0	1.6	27.8

a) Average compound growth rates.
b) See the main text for details of assumptions made in deriving these growth rates.
Source: Secretariat estimates.

Table B2. **The relationship between the growth rate of average real benefits and the share of social expenditure in GDP 1981-1990**

	Initial expenditure share (%) 1981	Policy Assumption — Fixed expenditure share: Growth rate of average real benefits (%)	Policy Assumption — Fixed expenditure share: Final expenditure share (%) 1990	Policy Assumption — No growth in average real benefits: Growth rate of average real benefits (%)	Policy Assumption — No growth in average real benefits: Final expenditure share (%) 1990	Policy Assumption — Growth in average real benefits based on the 1975-1981 trend: Growth rate of average real benefits (%)	Policy Assumption — Growth in average real benefits based on the 1975-1981 trend: Final expenditure share (%) 1990
Australia	16.9	0.2	16.9	0.0	16.6	-0.8	15.5
Finland	20.9	2.3	20.9	0.0	17.1	2.8	21.9
Ireland	23.2	-1.7	23.2	0.0	27.0	2.3	33.1
Netherlands	27.8	0.0	27.8	0.0	27.8	1.7	32.4
New Zealand	17.1	-1.5	17.1	0.0	19.6	0.6	20.6
Norway	20.7	1.7	20.7	0.0	17.8	2.9	23.0
Sweden	27.3	1.6	27.3	0.0	24.1	2.1	29.1

Sources: Tables A1, A7 and B1.

Annex C

OECD SOCIAL EXPENDITURE STATISTICS

This annex contains a full listing of OECD *Social Expenditure Statistics* as of 1st April 1984. Definitions of the main expenditure categories and a list of main statistical sources are provided immediately below. Some statistics have been taken from OECD *National Accounts* or have been supplied by national governments from unpublished sources. National governments and the OECD Secretariat have provided estimates when statistics have been missing. Secretariat estimates are indicated at the end of the annex.

Definitions

Only general definitions are provided here. These are a summary of those included in the "Instructions and Definitions" which accompany the Government Expenditure Questionnaire completed by Member governments, the response to which provides the basis of the government expenditure accounts included in OECD *National Accounts*. As these definitions are fairly broad, there is some variation between countries in the way in which expenditures are allocated between categories.

Education

Expenditure on pre-primary, primary, secondary, tertiary, education affairs and services and subsidiary services to education.

Health

Expenditure on hospitals, clinics and medical, dental and para-medical practitioners, public health, medicaments, prostheses, medical equipment and appliances or other prescribed health-related products, and applied research and experimental development related to health and medical delivery systems.

Pensions

Expenditure on old-age, disability or survivors' benefits, other than for government employees, and government employee pensions.

Unemployment Compensation

Expenditure on social insurance and other government schemes to individuals to compensate for loss of income due to unemployment.

Other Social Expenditure

Expenditure on sickness, maternity or temporary disablement benefits, family and child allowances, other social assistance and welfare affairs and services.

Total Social Expenditure

The total of the above five categories.

Total Government Expenditure

Expenditure by general government i.e. **central government, state or** provincial government, local government and social security funds.

Expenditure includes current outlays **and capital outlays.**

Main Statistical Sources

Canada

Consolidated Government Finance.
National Income and Expenditure Accounts.

France

Eurostat
Le Rapport sur les Comptes de la Nation, INSEE.
Les Comptes de la Protection Sociale, INSEE.
Les Comptes de la Santé, INSEE.

Germany

Eurostat
Volkswirtschaftlich Gesamtrechnungen, Fascherie 18.

Italy

Eurostat.
Relazione Generale sulla Situazione Economica del Paese, ISTAT.
Annuario Statistico dell'Assistenza e della Previdenza Sociale.
La Spesa Previdenziale e i suoi effetti sulla Finanza Pubblica.

Japan

Annual Report on National Accounts.

United Kingdom

Eurostat.
National Income and Expenditure.
Annual Abstract of Statistics.

United States

National Income and Product Accounts.
Survey of Current Business.

Australia

Australian National Accounts.
Commonwealth Government Finance.

Austria

Oesterreichs Volkseinkommen.
Statistiches Handbuch.

Belgium

Bulletin de Statistiques.
Annuaire Statistique.

Denmark

Statistisk Tiarsoversigt.
Statistiske Efterretninger.
Danmarks Statistik.

Finland

Statistical Yearbook of Finland
Statistical Yearbook of the Social Insurance Institution.
Economic Survey of Finland.
Social Expenditure in 1980

Greece

National Accounts of Greece.

Ireland

National Income and Expenditure.
Report of the Department of Social Welfare 1979-80.
Public Social Expenditure Trends in Ireland, Budget 1983.

Netherlands

Nationale Rekeningen.

New Zealand

New Zealand Yearbook.
Monthly Abstract of Statistics.
Public Expenditure and Its Financing: 1950-79.

Norway

Nasjonal Regnskap.
Statistisk Arbok.
Yearbook of Nordic Statistics.

Sweden

Statistisk Arsbok.
Statistiska Meddelanden.

Switzerland

Annuaire Statistique de la Suisse.

Note: The following statistics are Secretariat estimates.

Canada:	(1) 1960-64, 1981.
	(2) 1960-69, 1981.
France:	(1) 1960-81.
Germany:	(1) 1960-69.
Italy:	(1) 1960-69.
Japan:	(1) 1960-69.
	(2) 1960-64.
United Kingdom:	(1) 1960-69.
United States:	(1) 1960-69.
	(2) 1960-69.
Australia:	(1) 1960-65.
Austria:	(1) 1960-81.
Belgium:	(1) 1960-69.
Denmark:	(1) 1960-69, 1980, 1981.
Finland:	(1) 1960-69. 1978-81.
Greece:	(1) 1960-80.
	(2) 1960-80.

Ireland:	(1) 1960-62, 1980, 1981.
	(2) 1960-69, 1980, 1981.
New Zealand:	(1) 1960-81.
Norway:	(1) 1960-65.
	(2) 1960.
	(3) 1960, 1961.
Sweden:	(1) 1960-63, 1980, 1981.
	(2) 1960-81.
Switzerland:	(1) 1960, 1961.

Immediately prior to this book being sent to the printer the Italian and Greek authorities supplied the Secretariat with some revised social expenditure statistics. This annex does not incorporate these revisions. Growth rates and expenditure shares reported in the text are only slightly different from those based on the revised statistics, and the qualitative conclusions of the report are not affected by this change. The revised statistics, which will form the basis of any future work in this area, are available from the Secretariat.

CANADA (In millions of Canadian Dollars)

	1960	1961	1962	1963	1964	1965	1966	1967	1968	1969	1970	1971	1972	1973	1974	1975	1976	1977	1978	1979	1980	1981
AT CURRENT PRICES:																						
Education[1]	1 168	1 317	1 612	1 894	2 226	2 615	3 481	4 115	4 716	5 403	5 993	6 538	6 953	7 303	8 792	10 654	12 190	13 848	14 951	16 459	18 251	21 041
Health	922	1 045	1 173	1 339	1 527	1 719	2 129	2 551	3 074	3 650	4 392	5 218	5 786	6 455	7 677	9 478	10 873	11 872	12 935	14 323	16 506	19 126
Pensions	1 067	1 123	1 301	1 370	1 538	1 621	1 750	2 059	2 250	2 494	2 804	3 178	3 696	4 404	5 282	6 333	7 608	8 532	9 793	11 447	13 459	15 664
Unemployment comp.	563	603	527	524	483	468	527	709	950	1 094	1 441	1 861	2 864	3 084	3 349	4 610	4 994	5 781	6 576	6 309	6 926	7 933
Other social exp.[2]	981	1 015	1 079	1 104	1 140	1 212	1 276	1 356	1 448	1 557	1 562	1 929	2 106	3 051	4 668	5 213	5 707	6 423	6 316	7 083	8 424	9 533
Total social exp.	4 701	5 103	5 692	6 231	6 914	7 635	9 163	10 790	12 438	14 198	16 192	18 724	21 405	24 297	29 768	36 288	41 372	46 456	50 571	55 621	63 566	73 297
Total government exp.	11 342	12 157	13 133	13 827	14 788	16 431	19 004	21 709	24 340	27 080	30 982	34 941	39 451	44 662	55 547	67 724	76 081	85 555	95 980	105 541	120 809	140 273
GDP	38 720	40 115	43 433	46 542	50 884	56 040	62 597	67 258	73 325	80 493	86 454	95 365	106 005	124 506	148 891	166 751	194 117	213 382	236 596	270 061	302 985	348 574
AT 1970 PRICES:																						
Education[1]	1 921	2 097	2 507	2 896	3 212	3 612	4 503	4 988	5 402	5 717	5 993	6 162	6 110	5 913	6 131	6 437	6 501	6 732	6 711	6 818	6 688	6 823
Health	1 151	1 300	1 432	1 613	1 805	1 980	2 387	2 740	3 239	3 721	4 392	5 271	5 645	5 966	6 545	7 169	7 452	7 610	7 741	7 840	8 147	8 554
Pensions	1 361	1 423	1 628	1 689	1 873	1 937	2 025	2 306	2 419	2 582	2 804	3 107	3 470	3 860	4 166	4 517	5 055	5 267	5 628	6 022	6 397	6 691
Unemployment comp.	718	764	660	646	588	559	610	794	1 022	1 133	1 441	1 819	2 689	2 703	2 641	3 288	3 318	3 569	3 779	3 319	3 292	3 389
Other social exp.[2]	1 251	1 286	1 350	1 361	1 389	1 448	1 477	1 518	1 557	1 612	1 562	1 886	1 977	2 674	3 681	3 718	3 792	3 965	3 630	3 726	4 004	4 072
Total social exp.	6 402	6 870	7 577	8 205	8 867	9 536	11 002	12 346	13 639	14 765	16 192	18 245	19 891	21 116	23 164	25 129	26 118	27 143	27 489	27 725	28 528	29 529
Total government exp.	17 325	18 102	19 149	19 820	20 229	21 685	23 733	25 581	27 272	28 397	30 982	33 530	35 749	37 606	41 141	44 124	44 629	46 151	47 870	48 404	49 504	51 246
GDP	51 903	53 558	57 149	60 288	64 166	68 509	73 299	75 826	80 049	84 286	86 454	92 498	97 881	105 246	108 998	110 212	116 938	119 609	124 197	128 478	129 758	134 897
PRICE INDEXES (1970 = 1.0000)																						
Education	0.8010	0.8040	0.8190	0.8300	0.8460	0.8680	0.8920	0.9310	0.9490	0.9810	1.0000	0.9900	1.0250	1.0820	1.1730	1.3220	1.4590	1.5600	1.6710	1.8270	2.0260	2.2360
Health	0.7840	0.7890	0.7990	0.8110	0.8210	0.8370	0.8640	0.8930	0.9300	0.9660	1.0000	1.0230	1.0650	1.1410	1.2680	1.4020	1.5050	1.6200	1.7400	1.9010	2.1040	2.3410
Private consumption	0.6080	0.6280	0.6430	0.6540	0.6930	0.7240	0.7730	0.8250	0.8730	0.9450	1.0000	1.0610	1.1380	1.2350	1.4340	1.6550	1.8750	2.0570	2.2280	2.4140	2.7290	3.0840
Government consumption	0.7460	0.7500	0.7600	0.7720	0.7930	0.8180	0.8540	0.8870	0.9160	0.9550	1.0000	1.0310	1.0830	1.1830	1.3660	1.5130	1.6600	1.7840	1.9050	2.1020	2.3350	2.5840
Gross Domestic Product																						

FRANCE (In billions of Francs)

	1960	1961	1962	1963	1964	1965	1966	1967	1968	1969	1970
AT CURRENT PRICES :											
Education	7.4	9.0	11.0	13.3	15.7	17.4	19.8	22.1	23.2	28.9	34.0
Health											
Pensions	17.5	20.2	20.8	28.1	32.6	37.0	42.4	45.9	52.8	59.7	66.5
Unemployment comp.	0.5	0.6	0.7	2.1	1.1	1.3	1.6	1.7	2.2	2.5	2.5
Other social exp.[1]	14.4	15.1	17.1	19.7	21.5	24.0	23.0	24.6	25.6	27.2	27.5
Total social exp.											
Total government exp.	100.3	113.3	131.7	151.2	168.7	183.8	198.3	217.2	245.1	274.6	302.2
GDP	296.5	323.5	361.2	404.9	449.2	483.5	523.4	565.4	614.5	700.7	782.6
AT 1970 PRICES :											
Education	11.7	14.0	16.2	18.2	20.6	22.1	24.2	26.2	26.4	30.2	34.0
Health											
Pensions	26.6	29.7	33.4	37.4	41.9	46.4	51.6	54.2	59.4	62.7	66.5
Unemployment comp.	0.8	0.9	1.0	1.5	1.4	1.6	1.9	2.0	2.5	2.6	2.5
Other social exp.[1]	26.2	26.1	27.4	28.8	29.9	32.3	29.7	30.8	29.9	29.3	27.5
Total social exp.											
Total government exp.	171.2	185.2	201.9	213.7	227.6	240.8	250.1	265.4	281.9	292.8	302.2
GDP	455.3	480.3	512.4	539.8	575.0	602.4	633.8	663.5	691.8	740.1	782.6
PRICE INDEXES (1970 = 1.0000)											
Education	0.6298	0.6439	0.6792	0.7331	0.7662	0.7870	0.8180	0.8423	0.8785	0.9572	1.0000
Health											
Private consumption	0.6593	0.6814	0.7111	0.7514	0.7772	0.7971	0.8223	0.8471	0.8891	0.9520	1.0000
Government consumption	0.5486	0.5773	0.6218	0.6821	0.7182	0.7407	0.7723	0.7983	0.8571	0.9267	1.0000
Gross Domestic Product	0.6513	0.6734	0.7049	0.7501	0.7812	0.8026	0.8258	0.8521	0.8883	0.9467	1.0000

	1971	1972	1973	1974	1975	1976	1977	1978	1979	1980	1981
AT CURRENT PRICES :											
Education	39.0	44.9	51.5	60.5	84.3	97.3	110.9	124.4	138.7	158.3	176.4
Health					79.9	94.8	105.8	125.3	146.5	169.9	200.4
Pensions	73.8	84.3	97.0	116.5	122.2	173.7	205.0	239.3	276.2	319.3	368.6
Unemployment comp.	2.9	3.3	3.9	5.6	11.3	15.0	18.5	25.0	29.9	40.3	59.4
Other social exp.[1]	30.7	33.9	39.5	43.8	53.3	54.9	61.3	74.5	84.4	94.2	107.0
Total social exp.					350.9	435.7	501.5	588.7	675.7	782.0	911.8
Total government exp.	332.5	373.0	425.8	502.8	626.3	723.2	827.1	962.5	1 103.7	1 273.0	1 506.5
GDP	872.4	981.1	1 114.2	1 278.3	1 452.3	1 678.0	1 884.6	2 141.1	2 442.3	2 765.3	3 106.1
AT 1970 PRICES :											
Education	37.3	40.7	44.4	47.2	49.2	51.5	52.5	53.3	53.4	53.4	52.3
Health					55.1	58.9	61.2	66.3	71.3	74.8	79.7
Pensions	69.9	75.5	81.4	86.1	81.2	105.1	113.8	122.8	127.8	130.6	134.0
Unemployment comp.	2.8	3.0	3.3	4.1	7.5	9.1	10.3	12.8	13.8	16.5	21.6
Other social exp.[1]	28.5	29.3	31.0	29.4	35.4	33.2	34.0	38.1	39.1	38.5	38.9
Total social exp.					228.4	257.9	271.8	292.6	305.4	313.8	326.5
Total government exp.	311.6	328.3	345.8	355.1	389.1	410.0	426.0	452.7	470.1	479.5	502.9
GDP	824.9	873.6	920.4	950.2	952.0	1 001.2	1 031.7	1 070.8	1 106.2	1 118.1	1 121.4
PRICE INDEXES (1970 = 1.0000)											
Education	1.0467	1.1020	1.1610	1.2803	1.4489	1.6080	1.7300	1.8906	2.0537	2.2727	2.5150
Health											
Private consumption	1.0550	1.1159	1.1919	1.3527	1.5049	1.6520	1.8009	1.9583	2.1612	2.4446	2.7510
Government consumption	1.0786	1.1560	1.2732	1.4920	1.7133	1.8898	2.1120	2.3352	2.5980	2.9639	3.3714
Gross Domestic Product	1.0576	1.1231	1.2105	1.3453	1.5256	1.6760	1.8266	1.9995	2.2079	2.4731	2.7699

GERMANY (In billions of DM)

	1960	1961	1962	1963	1964	1965	1966	1967	1968	1969	1970
AT CURRENT PRICES :											
Education[1]	7.2	8.3	9.4	11.8	12.3	15.9	16.0	18.3	20.9	23.9	27.1
Health	9.5	10.7	11.9	12.9	13.8	15.8	18.4	19.2	21.5	23.9	28.6
Pensions	29.7	32.3	34.6	37.2	41.1	45.7	50.0	56.4	59.6	64.8	71.8
Unemployment comp.	0.3	0.6	0.8	1.4	1.0	1.0	0.9	2.3	2.0	1.6	2.1
Other social exp.[1]	15.3	16.3	18.0	19.8	20.1	24.5	24.5	25.1	26.6	28.8	29.4
Total social exp.	62.0	68.1	74.8	83.1	88.3	102.9	109.7	121.3	130.7	143.1	158.9
Total government exp.	95.0	106.3	120.5	134.0	145.7	162.3	174.2	185.6	203.0	222.6	251.6
GDP	302.7	331.7	360.8	382.4	420.2	459.2	488.2	494.3	533.3	597.0	675.3
AT 1970 PRICES :											
Education[1]	12.3	13.2	14.3	17.0	17.2	20.7	19.9	22.2	24.7	26.1	27.1
Health	16.3	17.1	18.2	18.5	19.3	20.6	22.8	23.4	25.4	26.2	28.6
Pensions	38.9	40.9	42.5	44.4	48.0	51.7	54.6	60.5	63.0	67.1	71.8
Unemployment comp.	0.4	0.7	1.0	1.6	1.2	1.1	0.9	2.5	2.2	1.7	2.1
Other social exp.[1]	20.0	20.6	22.1	23.7	23.4	27.7	26.7	26.9	28.1	29.8	29.4
Total social exp.	87.9	92.6	98.1	105.1	109.0	121.8	124.9	135.5	143.4	150.9	158.9
Total government exp.	144.2	153.8	167.7	178.1	189.1	199.4	205.1	213.6	228.6	238.0	251.6
GDP	431.7	453.7	473.8	488.6	521.5	550.4	564.8	564.3	597.6	642.3	675.3
PRICE INDEXES (1970 = 1.0000)											
Education	0.6461	0.6422	0.6904	0.7072	0.7229	0.7639	0.8296	0.8576	0.9036	0.9380	1.0000
Health	0.7639	0.7898	0.8139	0.8381	0.8575	0.8849	0.9165	0.9315	0.9466	0.9660	1.0000
Private consumption	0.5851	0.6234	0.6574	0.6969	0.7165	0.7659	0.8045	0.8238	0.8476	0.9135	1.0000
Government consumption											
Gross Domestic Product	0.7012	0.7312	0.7614	0.7826	0.8057	0.8342	0.8644	0.8761	0.8923	0.9294	1.0000

	1971	1972	1973	1974	1975	1976	1977	1978	1979	1980	1981
AT CURRENT PRICES :											
Education[1]	33.6	38.5	43.9	50.7	55.4	56.6	59.6	63.5	68.9	75.8	79.8
Health	35.1	40.7	49.3	58.6	67.6	71.9	75.7	81.4	87.9	96.7	100.8
Pensions	79.5	90.0	101.4	116.7	132.1	148.0	160.8	166.4	175.0	184.3	193.7
Unemployment comp.	2.0	2.4	3.1	6.1	12.3	11.1	10.6	10.8	12.7	13.5	21.0
Other social exp.[1]	36.5	41.3	43.9	50.2	66.7	68.8	71.0	74.9	78.4	85.7	90.9
Total social exp.	186.7	212.8	241.6	282.2	334.2	356.4	377.7	396.9	423.0	456.0	486.2
Total government exp.	288.7	323.5	367.7	423.2	486.1	517.7	551.6	592.0	639.1	689.6	736.7
GDP	750.6	823.7	917.3	984.6	1 026.5	1 119.7	1 196.1	1 285.1	1 392.5	1 481.4	1 542.6
AT 1970 PRICES :											
Education[1]	29.7	31.8	33.0	34.0	34.9	34.3	34.5	35.5	36.9	38.2	38.3
Health	31.0	33.6	37.0	39.3	42.6	43.6	43.9	45.5	47.0	48.7	48.3
Pensions	75.4	80.9	85.1	91.4	97.6	104.9	110.1	110.8	111.9	111.8	110.8
Unemployment comp.	1.9	2.2	2.6	4.7	9.1	7.9	7.2	7.2	8.1	8.2	12.0
Other social exp.[1]	34.6	37.1	36.9	39.3	49.3	48.8	48.6	49.9	50.1	51.9	52.0
Total social exp.	172.6	185.5	194.6	208.7	233.4	239.4	244.4	249.0	254.1	258.8	261.3
Total government exp.	262.6	277.0	289.3	303.2	329.1	337.2	345.1	358.1	369.7	376.5	381.4
GDP	696.2	725.1	758.1	762.2	749.3	790.4	814.6	839.7	874.8	890.9	890.2
PRICE INDEXES (1970 = 1.0000)											
Education	1.0887	1.1741	1.2410	1.3582	1.4676	1.5517	1.6172	1.6781	1.7524	1.8572	..
Health	1.0544	1.1133	1.1905	1.2770	1.3538	1.4103	1.4605	1.5013	1.5634	1.6495	1.7485
Private consumption	1.1325	1.2093	1.3316	1.4914	1.5881	1.6504	1.7261	1.7872	1.8697	1.9849	2.0858
Government consumption											
Gross Domestic Product	1.0781	1.1360	1.2099	1.2918	1.3700	1.4166	1.4683	1.5304	1.5918	1.6628	1.7329

81

JAPAN (In 10 billions of Yen)

	1960	1961	1962	1963	1964	1965	1966	1967	1968	1969	1970
AT CURRENT PRICES :											
Education[1]	62.8	72.4	83.7	95.8	111.7	129.0	149.0	172.1	197.9	227.6	262.9
Health[2]	21.0	40.0	48.0	59.0	73.0	88.4	104.5	126.3	149.3	172.4	216.4
Pensions	22.0	24.7	26.7	29.9	34.3	39.2	45.7	53.7	63.8	72.4	88.6
Unemployment comp.	4.0	4.9	7.3	9.8	10.0	11.6	12.6	12.9	13.9	15.2	20.2
Other social exp.[1]	17.1	20.0	24.1	29.1	35.5	41.1	49.0	60.1	66.8	78.6	94.3
Total social exp.	126.9	162.0	189.8	223.6	264.5	309.3	360.8	425.1	491.7	566.2	682.4
Total government exp.	269.3	330.9	390.9	456.4	536.6	610.3	718.5	805.5	959.8	1 114.1	1 425.1
GDP	1 584.1	1 957.9	2 171.5	2 507.6	2 964.6	3 275.0	3 802.9	4 456.7	5 285.3	6 218.1	7 328.5
AT 1970 PRICES :											
Education[1]	148.1	156.0	168.4	177.7	189.0	201.2	216.6	234.5	247.1	257.8	262.9
Health[2]	49.5	86.2	96.6	109.5	123.5	137.9	151.9	172.1	186.4	195.2	216.4
Pensions	38.5	40.8	41.6	43.6	47.9	51.2	57.0	63.9	71.9	77.9	88.6
Unemployment comp.	7.0	8.1	11.4	14.3	14.0	15.2	15.7	15.3	15.7	16.4	20.2
Other social exp.[1]	29.9	33.1	37.5	42.4	49.6	53.7	61.1	71.5	75.3	84.6	94.3
Total social exp.	273.0	324.2	355.5	387.5	424.0	459.2	502.3	557.3	596.4	631.9	682.4
Total government exp.	608.8	688.2	760.1	819.4	884.4	928.8	1 022.2	1 075.6	1 180.8	1 252.4	1 425.1
GDP	2 666.8	3 054.4	3 270.3	3 613.3	4 094.8	4 303.5	4 759.6	5 274.2	5 945.2	6 671.8	7 328.5
PRICE INDEXES (1970 = 1.0000)											
Education	:	:	:	:	:	:	:	0.8410	0.8870	0.9290	1.0000
Health	:	:	:	:	:	:	:	0.7340	0.8010	0.8830	1.0000
Private consumption	0.5720	0.6050	0.6420	0.6860	0.7160	0.7650	0.8020	0.8410	0.8870	0.9290	1.0000
Government consumption	0.4240	0.4640	0.4970	0.5390	0.5910	0.6410	0.6880	0.7340	0.8010	0.8830	0.9320
Gross Domestic Product	0.5940	0.6410	0.6640	0.6940	0.7240	0.7610	0.7990	0.8450	0.8890	0.9320	1.0000

	1971	1972	1973	1974	1975	1976	1977	1978	1979	1980	1981
AT CURRENT PRICES :											
Education[1]	312.1	364.6	449.3	625.0	725.2	802.5	892.2	1 009.6	1 087.1	1 174.2	1 251.3
Health[2]	240.2	290.2	350.0	495.3	589.4	691.6	766.2	913.0	984.6	1 094.1	1 172.1
Pensions	105.1	127.4	170.8	270.3	393.1	538.6	665.1	791.5	896.6	1 043.7	1 191.2
Unemployment comp.	26.6	31.4	35.0	51.0	70.6	67.7	75.4	87.5	86.1	95.4	110.5
Other social exp.[1]	110.6	148.0	195.1	268.4	326.2	367.2	417.3	481.6	534.5	584.3	638.2
Total social exp.	794.6	961.6	1 200.2	1 710.0	2 104.5	2 467.6	2 816.2	3 283.2	3 588.9	3 991.7	4 363.3
Total government exp.	1 690.7	2 042.0	2 468.9	3 331.4	3 902.5	4 445.5	5 115.3	5 887.2	6 450.3	7 098.1	7 658.9
GDP	8 063.2	9 230.6	11 242.0	13 416.9	14 803.1	16 585.1	18 446.0	20 263.8	21 861.6	23 591.2	25 180.7
AT 1970 PRICES :											
Education[1]	279.4	292.6	305.6	335.5	341.6	357.0	371.0	407.3	420.4	423.9	434.8
Health[2]	215.0	232.9	238.1	265.9	277.6	307.7	318.6	368.3	380.7	395.0	407.3
Pensions	98.7	113.5	137.6	178.9	233.0	293.4	338.1	384.6	420.9	458.2	500.1
Unemployment comp.	25.0	28.0	28.2	33.8	41.8	36.9	38.3	42.5	40.4	41.9	46.4
Other social exp.[1]	103.8	131.9	157.2	177.6	193.4	200.0	212.2	234.0	250.3	256.5	267.9
Total social exp.	721.9	798.9	866.7	991.7	1 087.4	1 195.0	1 278.2	1 436.7	1 513.3	1 575.5	1 656.5
Total government exp.	1 524.1	1 666.0	1 729.8	1 862.0	1 934.4	2 074.8	2 234.2	2 487.1	2 619.8	2 696.9	2 801.6
GDP	7 664.6	8 333.4	9 073.4	8 980.5	9 194.5	9 681.9	10 191.2	10 698.9	11 251.5	11 789.7	12 241.5
PRICE INDEXES (1970 = 1.0000)											
Education	1.1320	1.2930	1.5560	2.0050	2.1970	2.3380	2.4860	2.5670	2.6870	2.8670	:
Health	1.0960	1.2130	1.4220	1.8400	2.0160	2.1530	2.2890	2.3290	2.4260	2.5810	2.3820
Private consumption	1.0650	1.1220	1.2410	1.5110	1.6870	1.8360	1.9670	2.0580	2.1300	2.2780	2.8780
Government consumption	1.1170	1.2460	1.4700	1.8630	2.1230	2.2480	2.4050	2.4790	2.5860	2.7700	2.0570
Gross Domestic Product	1.0520	1.1070	1.2390	1.4940	1.6100	1.7130	1.8100	1.8940	1.9430	2.0010	

ITALY (In billions of Lire)

	1960	1961	1962	1963	1964	1965	1966	1967	1968	1969	1970
AT CURRENT PRICES:											
Education[1]	865	973	1 095	1 232	1 386	1 559	1 754	1 974	2 220	2 498	2 810
Health	744	851	956	1 192	1 392	1 590	1 790	2 050	2 263	2 541	3 006
Pensions	1 266	1 351	1 642	2 081	2 323	3 013	3 382	3 507	4 085	4 526	5 125
Unemployment comp.	43	60	67	64	83	125	100	90	98	118	112
Other social exp.[1]	986	1 049	1 347	1 397	1 415	1 595	1 648	1 916	1 936	2 314	2 409
Total social exp.	3 904	4 284	5 107	5 966	6 599	7 882	8 674	9 537	10 602	11 997	13 462
Total government exp.	6 928	7 451	8 624	10 182	11 431	13 138	14 260	15 265	17 178	18 632	20 970
GDP	23 207	25 810	28 998	33 215	36 360	39 124	42 391	46 695	50 614	55 876	62 883
AT 1970 PRICES:											
Education[1]	1 717	1 823	1 842	1 774	1 841	1 898	2 083	2 293	2 488	2 655	2 810
Health	1 477	1 595	1 608	1 716	1 849	1 935	2 126	2 381	2 536	2 701	3 006
Pensions	1 837	1 927	2 223	2 632	2 800	3 507	3 825	3 845	4 414	4 753	5 125
Unemployment comp.	62	86	91	81	100	146	113	99	106	124	112
Other social exp.[1]	1 431	1 496	1 824	1 767	1 706	1 857	1 864	2 101	2 092	2 430	2 409
Total social exp.	6 524	6 927	7 588	7 970	8 296	9 343	10 011	10 719	11 636	12 663	13 462
Total government exp.	12 528	12 862	13 505	14 041	14 715	15 740	16 646	17 372	19 007	19 716	20 970
GDP	36 092	39 053	41 479	43 808	45 028	46 504	49 286	52 822	56 282	59 709	62 883
PRICE INDEXES (1970 = 1.0000)											
Education	..	..	..	..	..	..	..	..	..	..	1.0000
Health	..	..	..	..	..	..	..	..	..	..	1.0000
Private consumption	0.6892	0.7011	0.7385	0.7906	0.8295	0.8591	0.8842	0.9121	0.9254	0.9522	1.0000
Government consumption	0.5037	0.5336	0.5944	0.6945	0.7528	0.8216	0.8419	0.8610	0.8922	0.9408	1.0000
Gross Domestic Product	0.6430	0.6609	0.6991	0.7582	0.8075	0.8413	0.8601	0.8840	0.8993	0.9358	1.0000

	1971	1972	1973	1974	1975	1976	1977	1978	1979	1980	1981
AT CURRENT PRICES:											
Education[1]	3 348	3 811	4 591	5 130	6 209	7 793	9 760	11 345	14 316	19 022	25 532
Health	3 581	4 218	5 062	6 412	7 260	9 114	10 487	13 193	16 183	20 319	23 923
Pensions	5 956	7 152	8 525	9 935	13 015	16 939	20 920	26 961	31 612	40 093	52 590
Unemployment comp.	193	204	235	406	561	714	787	1 058	1 364	1 589	2 589
Other social exp.[1]	2 695	3 012	3 334	4 648	5 534	6 265	6 454	7 687	8 178	9 932	11 181
Total social exp.	15 773	18 397	21 747	26 531	32 579	40 825	48 408	60 244	71 653	90 955	115 815
Total government exp.	24 501	28 082	32 434	39 118	52 128	63 224	77 056	96 298	113 825	142 843	180 620
GDP	68 510	75 124	89 746	110 719	125 378	156 657	190 083	222 254	270 198	338 743	401 300
AT 1970 PRICES:											
Education[1]	2 889	3 042	3 260	3 116	3 360	3 607	3 706	3 624	3 732	3 994	4 215
Health	3 090	3 367	3 594	3 894	3 929	4 219	3 982	4 214	4 219	4 267	3 950
Pensions	5 643	6 368	6 747	6 502	7 240	7 979	8 337	9 517	9 696	10 227	11 275
Unemployment comp.	183	182	186	266	312	336	314	373	418	405	555
Other social exp.[1]	2 554	2 682	2 638	3 042	3 079	2 951	2 572	2 713	2 508	2 533	2 397
Total social exp.	14 359	15 641	16 425	16 820	17 920	19 092	18 911	20 441	20 573	21 426	22 392
Total government exp.	21 891	23 372	24 013	24 465	28 500	29 460	29 789	31 957	31 567	32 322	33 092
GDP	63 915	65 962	70 599	73 523	70 851	75 009	76 434	88 488	82 337	85 558	85 678
PRICE INDEXES (1970 = 1.0000)											
Education	1.1434	1.2534	1.4630	1.5713	1.7971	2.1671	2.7446	3.1815	3.8584	4.8101	
Health	1.0515	1.0890	1.1678	1.2928	1.5210	1.7201	1.9025	2.1757	2.4266	3.0400	3.7412
Private consumption	1.0554	1.1231	1.2636	1.5279	1.7976	2.1230	2.5094	2.8329	3.2604	3.9205	4.6641
Government consumption	1.1588	1.2527	1.4084	1.6465	1.8477	2.1603	2.6336	3.1309	3.8359	4.7621	6.0568
Gross Domestic Product	1.0719	1.1389	1.2712	1.5059	1.7696	2.0885	2.4869	2.8317	3.2816	3.9592	4.6838

UNITED KINGDOM (In millions of Pounds Sterling)

	1960	1961	1962	1963	1964	1965	1966	1967	1968	1969	1970
AT CURRENT PRICES :											
Education	932	1 030	1 192	1 298	1 436	1 606	1 795	2 003	2 207	2 372	2 719
Health	861	930	971	1 035	1 130	1 274	1 407	1 558	1 693	1 770	2 020
Pensions	1 048	1 161	1 228	1 379	1 515	1 765	1 895	2 046	2 286	2 416	2 656
Unemployment comp.	62	60	88	133	87	84	90	192	216	207	241
Other social exp.[1]	653	719	774	866	928	1 044	1 133	1 260	1 502	1 689	1 838
Total social exp.	3 556	3 900	4 253	4 711	5 096	5 773	6 320	7 059	7 904	8 454	9 474
Total government exp.	8 477	9 254	9 902	10 560	11 358	12 507	13 608	15 334	16 828	17 611	19 372
GDP	25 691	27 414	28 693	30 508	33 272	35 740	38 073	40 273	43 682	46 656	51 175
AT 1970 PRICES :											
Education	1 617	1 715	1 910	2 008	2 121	2 221	2 343	2 498	2 601	2 628	2 719
Health	1 194	1 242	1 277	1 360	1 427	1 607	1 704	1 838	1 901	1 903	2 020
Pensions	1 550	1 668	1 698	1 870	1 983	2 203	2 274	2 392	2 556	2 559	2 656
Unemployment comp.	92	86	122	180	114	105	108	225	241	219	241
Other social exp.[1]	966	1 033	1 070	1 174	1 215	1 303	1 360	1 473	1 679	1 789	1 838
Total social exp.	5 419	5 744	6 077	6 592	6 860	7 439	7 789	8 426	8 978	9 098	9 474
Total government exp.	13 959	14 660	15 127	15 641	16 111	16 753	17 301	18 747	19 495	19 244	19 372
GDP	38 750	40 015	40 407	42 115	44 298	45 321	46 183	47 447	49 425	50 071	51 175
PRICE INDEXES (1970 = 1.0000)											
Education	0.5762	0.6005	0.6242	0.6464	0.6769	0.7230	0.7662	0.8018	0.8485	0.9025	1.0000
Health	0.7214	0.7488	0.7601	0.7611	0.7920	0.7929	0.8259	0.8478	0.8906	0.9302	1.0000
Private consumption	0.6762	0.6960	0.7233	0.7375	0.7639	0.8012	0.8332	0.8552	0.8945	0.9440	1.0000
Government consumption											
Gross Domestic Product	0.6630	0.6851	0.7101	0.7244	0.7511	0.7886	0.8244	0.8488	0.8838	0.9318	1.0000

	1971	1972	1973	1974	1975	1976	1977	1978	1979	1980	1981
AT CURRENT PRICES :											
Education	3 099	3 635	4 251	4 990	7 127	7 926	8 460	9 224	10 363	12 718	14 269
Health	2 295	2 646	3 008	3 939	5 261	6 232	6 929	7 868	9 077	11 787	13 419
Pensions	2 954	3 652	4 176	5 232	6 634	8 154	9 544	11 139	12 672	15 062	18 225
Unemployment comp.	353	460	306	432	733	1 172	1 384	1 410	1 383	2 127	3 426
Other social exp.[1]	1 905	2 065	2 383	2 838	3 801	4 728	5 440	6 915	8 627	8 174	9 338
Total social exp.	10 606	12 458	14 124	17 431	23 556	28 212	31 757	36 556	42 122	49 868	58 677
Total government exp.	21 423	24 597	28 831	36 800	47 928	56 286	61 834	70 199	81 994	100 522	116 060
GDP	57 441	63 552	73 273	83 396	105 118	125 266	144 372	166 030	193 924	226 242	249 233
AT 1970 PRICES :											
Education	2 799	3 002	3 208	3 078	3 356	3 236	3 127	3 088	3 041	3 009	2 975
Health	2 097	2 317	2 513	2 886	3 040	3 116	2 995	3 159	3 151	3 391	3 449
Pensions	2 722	3 157	3 322	3 545	3 638	3 866	3 929	4 214	4 245	4 346	4 741
Unemployment comp.	325	398	243	293	402	556	570	533	463	614	891
Other social exp.[1]	1 756	1 785	1 895	1 923	2 085	2 242	2 240	2 616	2 890	2 359	2 429
Total social exp.	9 699	10 659	11 181	11 725	12 521	13 016	12 861	13 610	13 790	13 719	14 485
Total government exp.	19 470	20 683	22 281	23 674	23 999	24 477	23 978	24 872	25 490	25 705	26 450
GDP	52 486	53 608	57 677	57 132	56 637	58 728	59 447	61 534	62 779	61 135	60 359
PRICE INDEXES (1970 = 1.0000)											
Education	1.1071	1.2110	1.3250	1.6210	2.1234	2.4495	2.7054	2.9874	3.4080	4.2261	4.7958
Health	1.0943	1.1419	1.1972	1.3651	1.7304	1.9999	2.3134	2.4906	2.8806	3.4764	3.8904
Private consumption	1.0851	1.1567	1.2572	1.4759	1.8234	2.1091	2.4290	2.6431	2.9855	3.4656	3.8440
Government consumption											
Gross Domestic Product	1.0944	1.1855	1.2704	1.4597	1.8560	2.1330	2.4286	2.6982	3.0890	3.7007	4.1292

UNITED STATES (In billions of Dollars)

	1960	1961	1962	1963	1964	1965	1966	1967	1968	1969	1970
AT CURRENT PRICES:											
Education[1]	18.2	20.2	22.5	24.9	27.7	30.7	34.1	37.8	42.0	47.0	52.2
Health	6.6	7.4	8.2	9.1	9.9	10.8	13.6	19.0	22.1	24.9	27.8
Pensions	21.2	23.4	25.4	27.2	28.5	31.3	34.0	36.9	41.4	45.1	52.6
Unemployment comp.	3.1	4.4	3.2	3.1	2.8	2.4	1.9	2.2	2.2	2.3	4.2
Other social exp.[2]	5.8	6.3	7.2	7.9	8.7	9.6	10.7	11.9	13.5	15.4	18.0
Total social exp.	54.9	61.7	66.5	72.2	77.6	84.8	94.3	107.8	121.2	134.7	154.8
Total government exp.	141.9	154.5	165.6	174.7	183.7	196.0	224.0	253.1	277.9	296.6	325.8
GDP	505.3	523.3	563.5	594.7	635.6	688.6	753.6	797.2	870.3	940.5	988.7
AT 1970 PRICES:											
Education[1]	27.9	30.1	32.6	35.0	37.9	40.8	43.1	45.7	48.2	51.0	52.2
Health	9.5	10.4	11.3	12.3	13.1	14.0	16.9	22.2	24.7	26.2	27.8
Pensions	27.3	29.8	31.9	33.6	34.7	37.4	39.6	41.9	45.2	47.1	52.6
Unemployment comp.	4.0	5.6	4.0	3.8	3.4	2.9	2.2	2.5	2.4	2.4	4.2
Other social exp.[2]	7.5	8.0	9.0	9.8	10.6	11.5	12.5	13.5	14.7	16.1	18.0
Total social exp.	76.2	83.9	88.8	94.5	99.7	106.6	114.3	125.8	135.2	142.8	154.8
Total government exp.	209.6	222.4	232.2	238.7	244.8	254.5	278.1	301.3	314.9	318.4	325.8
GDP	677.3	695.0	733.7	763.4	803.5	852.2	901.4	927.0	963.8	991.0	988.7
PRICE INDEXES (1970 = 1.0000)											
Education	0.6520	0.6700	0.6910	0.7110	0.7310	0.7520	0.7920	0.8230	0.8720	0.9220	1.0000
Health	0.6950	0.7130	0.7280	0.7390	0.7530	0.7730	0.8070	0.8540	0.8950	0.9510	1.0000
Private consumption	0.7760	0.7840	0.7970	0.8100	0.8220	0.8360	0.8590	0.8800	0.9160	0.9570	1.0000
Government consumption	0.6520	0.6700	0.6910	0.7110	0.7310	0.7520	0.7920	0.8230	0.8720	0.9220	1.0000
Gross Domestic Product	0.7460	0.7530	0.7680	0.7790	0.7910	0.8080	0.8360	0.8600	0.9030	0.9490	1.0000

	1971	1972	1973	1974	1975	1976	1977	1978	1979	1980	1981
AT CURRENT PRICES:											
Education[1]	61.7	68.1	75.1	84.4	97.5	104.3	111.2	122.1	133.2	148.0	159.6
Health	31.7	35.4	39.3	47.1	56.2	62.9	70.1	79.5	90.6	105.4	122.5
Pensions	60.7	68.0	81.1	92.3	106.0	119.2	131.9	144.7	162.6	186.7	215.4
Unemployment comp.	6.2	6.0	4.6	7.0	18.1	16.4	13.1	9.4	9.7	16.1	15.6
Other social exp.[2]	21.8	25.0	27.8	34.8	42.8	45.8	52.3	58.0	66.8	82.4	92.3
Total social exp.	182.1	202.5	227.9	265.6	320.6	348.6	378.6	413.7	462.9	538.6	605.4
Total government exp.	354.1	386.2	422.2	479.1	554.3	598.0	645.3	710.8	795.1	921.2	1 044.8
GDP	1 073.2	1 180.0	1 315.3	1 420.9	1 538.8	1 705.9	1 903.1	2 140.4	2 382.2	2 599.0	2 923.8
AT 1970 PRICES:											
Education[1]	57.7	59.5	61.5	63.7	67.5	67.8	67.3	68.9	69.7	70.0	69.0
Health	30.1	32.0	34.2	38.2	41.5	43.2	44.1	46.1	48.0	50.2	52.0
Pensions	58.0	62.7	70.6	73.0	77.8	83.0	86.7	88.9	91.7	95.3	101.0
Unemployment comp.	5.9	5.5	4.0	5.5	13.3	11.4	8.6	8.8	5.8	8.2	7.3
Other social exp.[2]	20.8	23.0	24.2	27.5	31.4	31.9	34.4	35.6	37.7	42.1	43.3
Total social exp.	172.5	182.7	194.5	207.9	231.5	237.3	241.1	245.3	252.6	265.8	272.6
Total government exp.	333.4	343.4	353.5	369.2	393.3	399.5	402.5	413.1	426.3	446.7	462.6
GDP	1 019.2	1 073.7	1 132.9	1 125.9	1 118.3	1 172.4	1 234.2	1 291.7	1 322.0	1 319.1	1 356.8
PRICE INDEXES (1970 = 1.0000)											
Education	1.0690	1.1440	1.2220	1.3240	1.4440	1.5380	1.6520	1.7710	1.9120	2.1150	2.3130
Health	1.0530	1.1050	1.1480	1.2320	1.3540	1.4560	1.5880	1.7250	1.8860	2.0990	2.3580
Private consumption	1.0460	1.0850	1.1480	1.2650	1.3620	1.4360	1.5220	1.6280	1.7740	1.9590	2.1320
Government consumption	1.0690	1.1440	1.2220	1.3240	1.4440	1.5380	1.6520	1.7710	1.9120	2.1150	2.3130
Gross Domestic Product	1.0530	1.0990	1.1610	1.2620	1.3760	1.4550	1.5420	1.6570	1.8020	1.9700	2.1520

AUSTRALIA (In millions of Australian Dollars)

	1960	1961	1962	1963	1964	1965	1966	1967	1968	1969	1970
AT CURRENT PRICES:											
Education[1]	410	463	495	555	632	719	792	886	1 002	1 179	1 406
Health	358	400	462	492	543	591	638	632	772	900	1 067
Pensions	493	547	571	622	654	692	730	772	847	958	1 032
Unemployment comp.	9	25	21	13	7	8	11	11	9	9	11
Other social exp.[1]	220	209	213	261	268	277	308	304	321	359	376
Total social exp.	1 490	1 644	1 762	1 943	2 104	2 287	2 479	2 605	2 951	3 405	3 892
Total government exp.	3 322	3 646	3 905	4 308	4 794	5 391	5 959	6 515	7 068	7 827	8 782
GDP	14 617	14 966	16 179	17 970	19 767	20 767	22 865	24 407	27 558	30 545	33 737
AT 1970 PRICES:											
Education[1]	627	691	723	788	848	928	984	1 044	1 138	1 272	1 406
Health	548	597	674	699	729	763	792	744	877	971	1 067
Pensions	648	703	732	787	806	824	844	864	921	1 006	1 032
Unemployment comp.	12	32	27	16	9	10	13	12	10	9	11
Other social exp.[1]	289	269	273	330	330	330	356	340	349	377	376
Total social exp.	2 124	2 292	2 429	2 620	2 722	2 855	2 989	3 004	3 295	3 635	3 892
Total government exp.	4 927	5 281	5 557	5 978	6 331	6 862	7 311	7 610	7 972	8 407	8 782
GDP	19 419	19 615	21 006	22 684	24 141	24 749	26 366	27 424	29 997	31 801	33 737
PRICE INDEXES (1970 = 1.0000)											
Education	..	..	..	..	0.7091	0.7234	0.7612	0.7998	0.8247	0.8915	1.0000
Health	..	..	..	..	0.7181	0.7519	0.7678	0.8184	0.8583	0.9118	1.0000
Private consumption	0.7607	0.7777	0.7804	0.7908	0.8117	0.8400	0.8648	0.8933	0.9201	0.9522	1.0000
Government consumption	0.6536	0.6699	0.6850	0.7042	0.7453	0.7746	0.8052	0.8489	0.8803	0.9267	1.0000
Gross Domestic Product	0.7527	0.7630	0.7702	0.7922	0.8188	0.8391	0.8672	0.8900	0.9187	0.9605	1.0000

	1971	1972	1973	1974	1975	1976	1977	1978	1979	1980	1981
AT CURRENT PRICES:											
Education[1]	1 665	1 986	2 523	3 716	4 477	5 132	5 763	6 185	6 704	7 593	8 634
Health	1 269	1 450	1 827	2 612	4 052	4 266	4 452	4 949	5 361	6 153	7 029
Pensions	1 192	1 527	2 023	2 803	3 676	4 329	5 127	5 696	6 302	7 267	8 371
Unemployment comp.	26	47	58	303	515	618	794	910	925	996	1 224
Other social exp.[1]	429	525	580	746	975	1 768	1 921	1 986	2 134	2 320	2 669
Total social exp.	4 581	5 535	7 011	10 180	13 695	16 113	18 057	19 726	21 426	24 329	27 927
Total government exp.	10 022	11 439	13 926	18 904	23 673	27 517	31 088	34 342	37 959	40 027	45 850
GDP	37 680	42 907	51 366	61 773	72 826	83 165	90 340	102 163	114 757	130 817	147 938
AT 1970 PRICES:											
Education[1]	1 489	1 641	1 854	2 254	2 243	2 254	2 306	2 314	2 331	2 361	2 413
Health	1 135	1 198	1 342	1 584	2 030	1 874	1 781	1 851	1 864	1 913	1 965
Pensions	1 112	1 341	1 634	1 954	2 195	2 265	2 426	2 485	2 508	2 627	2 779
Unemployment comp.	24	41	47	211	308	323	376	397	368	360	406
Other social exp.[1]	400	461	468	520	582	925	909	867	849	839	886
Total social exp.	4 160	4 682	5 345	6 523	7 358	7 641	7 798	7 914	7 920	8 100	8 449
Total government exp.	9 026	9 562	10 426	11 814	12 356	12 650	13 012	13 382	13 669	12 982	13 459
GDP	35 474	37 523	40 183	41 026	41 765	42 015	41 865	44 087	45 235	46 313	48 047
PRICE INDEXES (1970 = 1.0000)											
Education	1.0866	1.2001	1.3961	1.7108	1.9736	2.1887	2.3619	2.4968	2.7228	3.0687	..
Health	1.1036	1.1680	1.3747	1.7815	2.1232	2.4030	2.5800	2.7216	2.9347	3.2328	..
Private consumption	1.0724	1.1388	1.2382	1.4348	1.6746	1.9116	2.1133	2.2917	2.5132	2.7663	3.0120
Government consumption	1.1181	1.2099	1.3610	1.6487	1.9962	2.2768	2.4993	2.6730	2.8758	3.2157	3.5777
Gross Domestic Product	1.0622	1.1435	1.2783	1.5057	1.7437	1.9794	2.1579	2.3173	2.5369	2.8246	3.0790

AUSTRIA (In 10 millions of Schillings)

	1960	1961	1962	1963	1964	1965	1966	1967	1968	1969	1970	1971	1972	1973	1974	1975	1976	1977	1978	1979	1980	1981
AT CURRENT PRICES:																						
Education[1]	326	361	403	434	490	549	608	694	778	893	1 005	1 181	1 369	1 622	1 919	2 292	2 645	2 902	3 249	3 541	3 784	4 010
Health	470	520	560	620	669	750	830	950	980	1 140	1 260	1 390	1 580	1 830	2 240	2 670	3 200	3 410	3 760	4 110	4 500	4 940
Pensions	1 565	1 788	2 007	2 213	2 431	2 673	2 999	3 333	3 627	4 020	4 373	4 950	5 547	6 194	7 114	8 207	9 391	10 325	11 390	12 388	13 441	14 603
Unemployment comp.	53	48	57	66	76	89	85	94	117	118	108	115	118	117	195	253	289	303	372	431	440	566
Other social exp.[1]	499	510	609	672	727	785	834	918	815	1 068	1 364	1 541	1 816	2 039	2 339	2 627	2 856	3 250	4 225	4 553	4 814	5 175
Total social exp.	2 913	3 227	3 636	4 005	4 393	4 846	5 356	5 989	6 317	7 239	8 110	9 177	10 430	11 802	13 807	16 049	18 381	20 190	22 996	25 023	26 979	29 294
Total government exp.					8 227	8 998	9 933	11 101	12 012	13 146	14 359	16 275	18 461	20 975	24 826	28 977	32 748	36 107	40 670	43 821	47 104	51 015
GDP	16 287	18 034	19 190	20 684	22 661	24 632	26 826	28 544	30 671	33 490	37 588	41 962	47 954	54 346	61 856	65 612	72 475	79 619	84 233	91 854	99 697	105 885
AT 1970 PRICES:																						
Education[1]	633	656	691	695	751	777	808	846	899	946	1 005	1 087	1 160	1 211	1 273	1 363	1 450	1 518	1 589	1 659	1 683	1 662
Health	912	945	960	993	1 025	1 061	1 103	1 158	1 132	1 207	1 260	1 279	1 338	1 366	1 486	1 587	1 755	1 784	1 839	1 926	2 001	2 047
Pensions	2 194	2 413	2 605	2 784	2 972	3 133	3 433	3 675	3 899	4 182	4 373	4 715	4 962	5 198	5 427	5 803	6 233	6 504	6 877	7 163	7 296	7 395
Unemployment comp.	74	65	74	83	93	104	97	104	126	123	108	110	106	98	149	179	192	191	225	249	239	287
Other social exp.[1]	700	688	791	845	889	920	955	1 012	876	1 111	1 364	1 468	1 624	1 711	1 784	1 858	1 896	2 047	2 551	2 633	2 613	2 621
Total social exp.	4 513	4 767	5 121	5 400	5 730	5 995	6 396	6 795	6 932	7 569	8 110	8 659	9 190	9 584	10 119	10 790	11 525	12 044	13 081	13 630	13 832	14 012
Total government exp.					11 604	11 868	12 478	13 028	13 511	13 824	14 359	15 190	15 992	16 432	17 429	18 476	19 404	20 373	21 724	22 437	22 782	23 012
GDP	23 557	24 864	25 515	26 576	28 220	29 040	30 679	31 603	33 015	35 090	37 588	39 509	41 962	44 012	45 748	45 583	47 668	49 746	50 005	52 359	53 943	53 861
PRICE INDEXES (1970 = 1.0000)																						
Education																						
Health					0.6106	0.6506	0.6983	0.7613	0.8472	0.9119	1.0000	1.1107	1.2355	1.3445	1.5131	1.5729	1.9116	2.1457	2.2613	2.2299		
Private consumption	0.7132	0.7409	0.7703	0.7949	0.8179	0.8533	0.8737	0.9070	0.9303	0.9612	1.0000	1.0498	1.1179	1.1915	1.3108	1.4142	1.5067	1.5876	1.6563	1.7295	1.8422	1.9747
Government consumption	0.5154	0.5500	0.5836	0.6242	0.6527	0.7070	0.7526	0.8202	0.8656	0.9443	1.0000	1.0868	1.1806	1.3396	1.5074	1.6821	1.8238	1.9111	2.0450	2.1345	2.2486	2.4134
Gross Domestic Product	0.6914	0.7253	0.7521	0.7783	0.8030	0.8482	0.8744	0.9032	0.9290	0.9544	1.0000	1.0621	1.1428	1.2348	1.3521	1.4394	1.5204	1.6005	1.6845	1.7543	1.8482	1.9659

87

BELGIUM (In 10 millions of Francs)

	1960	1961	1962	1963	1964	1965	1966	1967	1968	1969	1970
AT CURRENT PRICES :											
Education[1]	2 486	2 809	3 113	3 514	3 857	4 414	5 032	5 570	5 957	6 717	7 569
Health	1 480	1 550	1 675	1 770	1 900	2 463	2 701	2 836	3 276	3 886	4 478
Pensions					3 320	3 780	4 320	4 720	5 710	6 250	7 290
Unemployment comp.				490	350	420	430	630	710	640	570
Other social exp.[1]	5 840	6 600	7 460	7 940	5 859	6 662	7 741	8 583	9 619	10 670	11 967
Total social exp.	9 806	10 959	12 248	13 714	15 286	17 739	20 224	22 339	25 272	28 163	31 874
Total government exp.	17 091	17 859	19 609	21 755	23 836	27 176	30 276	33 457	37 689	41 594	46 749
GDP	55 702	59 244	63 371	68 130	76 253	82 996	89 211	95 535	102 234	113 417	126 211
AT 1970 PRICES :											
Education[1]	3 567	4 027	4 399	4 870	5 167	5 609	6 075	6 463	6 626	7 143	7 569
Health	2 123	2 222	2 367	2 453	2 546	3 130	3 261	3 291	3 644	4 133	4 478
Pensions					4 023	4 378	4 804	5 119	6 019	6 406	7 290
Unemployment comp.				618	424	486	478	683	748	656	570
Other social exp.[1]	7 932	8 730	9 763	10 021	7 099	7 716	8 609	9 309	10 139	10 936	11 967
Total social exp.	13 622	14 979	16 529	17 962	19 259	21 319	23 227	24 865	27 176	29 274	31 874
Total government exp.	24 074	24 870	26 930	29 107	30 714	33 312	35 363	37 766	40 986	43 558	46 749
GDP	78 058	81 942	86 219	89 964	96 230	99 647	102 801	106 791	111 269	118 662	126 211
PRICE INDEXES (1970 = 1.0000)											
Education	0.6897	0.6909	0.6986	0.7101	0.7347	0.7802	0.8239	0.8578	0.8976	0.9406	1.0000
Health											
Private consumption	0.7363	0.7560	0.7641	0.7923	0.8253	0.8634	0.8992	0.9220	0.9487	0.9757	1.0000
Government consumption	0.6970	0.6976	0.7077	0.7215	0.7464	0.7869	0.8283	0.8618	0.8991	0.9403	1.0000
Gross Domestic Product	0.7136	0.7230	0.7350	0.7573	0.7924	0.8329	0.8678	0.8946	0.9188	0.9558	1.0000

	1971	1972	1973	1974	1975	1976	1977	1978	1979	1980	1981
AT CURRENT PRICES :											
Education[1]	8 737	10 141	11 294	14 011	17 650	20 076	21 378	23 044	24 780	27 296	29 713
Health	4 962	5 795	6 802	7 996	10 121	12 108	13 624	15 227	16 418	17 391	19 000
Pensions	8 450	9 960	11 900	14 610	18 250	21 270	23 490	25 840	28 470	31 240	:
Unemployment comp.	670	1 030	1 180	1 610	3 580	4 670	5 990	6 910	7 950	8 990	11 930
Other social exp.[1]	13 045	15 369	17 596	21 350	28 785	34 084	38 963	41 248	43 175	46 464	:
Total social exp.	35 864	42 295	48 772	59 577	78 386	92 208	103 445	112 269	120 793	130 999	:
Total government exp.	53 309	60 924	69 725	82 478	102 834	118 335	132 538	146 406	161 287	179 989	237 529
GDP	138 202	154 539	175 502	205 681	227 114	257 242	277 493	298 160	318 199	342 615	355 939
AT 1970 PRICES :											
Education[1]	8 024	8 560	8 814	9 545	10 194	10 610	10 478	10 782	11 015	11 262	11 353
Health	4 557	4 892	5 309	5 447	5 846	6 399	6 677	7 124	7 298	7 175	7 260
Pensions	8 032	8 978	10 116	11 061	12 281	13 302	13 722	14 488	15 385	15 781	:
Unemployment comp.	637	928	1 003	1 219	2 409	2 921	3 499	3 874	4 296	4 541	5 535
Other social exp.[1]	12 399	13 853	14 959	16 164	19 371	21 316	22 761	23 126	23 332	23 471	:
Total social exp.	33 649	37 211	40 201	43 436	50 101	54 548	57 137	59 394	61 326	62 080	:
Total government exp.	49 670	52 936	56 554	59 037	64 221	68 356	71 396	75 366	79 326	82 293	:
GDP	129 149	135 978	144 387	150 826	147 928	156 093	157 077	162 026	166 031	171 367	169 414
PRICE INDEXES (1970 = 1.0000)											
Education	1.0879	1.1905	1.2916	1.4854	1.7624	1.9098	2.0764	:	:	:	:
Health											
Private consumption	1.0521	1.1094	1.1763	1.3208	1.4860	1.5990	1.7118	1.7836	1.8505	1.9796	2.1555
Government consumption	1.0889	1.1847	1.2813	1.4679	1.7314	1.8921	2.0403	2.1373	2.2497	2.4237	2.6171
Gross Domestic Product	1.0701	1.1365	1.2155	1.3637	1.5353	1.6480	1.7666	1.8402	1.9165	1.9993	2.1010

DENMARK (In millions of Kroner)

	1960	1961	1962	1963	1964	1965	1966	1967	1968	1969	1970
AT CURRENT PRICES:											
Education	1 330	1 663	1 953	2 172	2 440	2 928	3 514	4 218	4 952	5 829	8 380
Health	1 905	2 143	2 418	2 714	2 960	3 511	4 070	4 688	5 446	6 021	6 208
Pensions	:	:	:	:	:	:	:	:	:	:	8 577
Unemployment comp.	140	146	190	183	120	172	154	431	625	526	496
Other social exp.[1]	:	:	:	:	:	:	:	:	:	:	7 410
Total social exp.	:	:	:	:	:	:	:	:	:	:	31 071
Total government exp.	:	:	:	:	:	:	:	:	:	:	49 092
GDP	41 149	45 659	51 448	54 765	62 601	70 320	77 183	84 813	94 358	107 319	118 627
AT 1970 PRICES:											
Education	3 207	3 499	3 811	4 030	4 216	4 446	4 898	5 523	5 848	6 375	8 380
Health	3 350	3 640	3 869	4 112	4 313	4 824	5 250	5 664	6 111	6 451	6 208
Pensions	:	:	:	:	:	:	:	:	:	:	8 577
Unemployment comp.	246	248	304	277	175	236	199	521	701	564	496
Other social exp.[1]	:	:	:	:	:	:	:	:	:	:	7 410
Total social exp.	:	:	:	:	:	:	:	:	:	:	31 071
Total government exp.	:	:	:	:	:	:	:	:	:	:	49 092
GDP	76 202	81 056	85 661	86 203	94 193	98 487	101 184	104 889	108 896	115 995	118 627
PRICE INDEXES (1970 = 1.0000)											
Education	:	:	:	:	:	:	:	:	:	:	:
Health	:	:	:	:	:	:	:	:	:	0.8759	1.0000
Private consumption	0.5686	0.5888	0.6250	0.6600	0.6863	0.7278	0.7118	0.7733	0.8173	0.9144	1.0000
Government consumption	0.4147	0.4753	0.5125	0.5389	0.5787	0.6586	0.7753	0.8277	0.8912	0.9334	1.0000
Gross Domestic Product	0.5400	0.5633	0.6006	0.6353	0.6646	0.7140	0.7628	0.8086	0.8665	0.9252	1.0000

	1971	1972	1973	1974	1975	1976	1977	1978	1979	1980	1981
AT CURRENT PRICES:											
Education	9 862	11 452	12 565	15 445	17 599	18 975	20 855	23 369	26 599	:	:
Health	7 204	8 196	9 072	11 165	12 841	14 629	15 543	17 416	19 425	21 645	24 035
Pensions	9 545	10 872	12 520	14 626	16 855	18 561	20 814	23 881	26 990	30 073	33 335
Unemployment comp.	843	764	789	2 838	5 151	5 682	7 774	9 930	11 862	15 223	20 848
Other social exp.[1]	8 799	10 750	12 478	15 328	17 601	19 770	22 275	26 345	30 588	:	:
Total social exp.	36 253	42 034	47 424	59 402	70 047	77 617	87 261	100 941	115 464	:	:
Total government exp.	56 297	63 797	70 901	90 467	102 879	114 589	127 811	147 075	186 674	:	:
GDP	131 120	150 729	172 860	193 629	216 256	251 214	279 310	311 376	346 892	373 786	410 579
AT 1970 PRICES:											
Education	8 837	9 427	9 373	9 700	9 594	9 496	9 688	10 095	10 681	:	:
Health	6 455	6 747	6 767	7 012	7 000	7 321	7 220	7 523	7 800	7 879	7 868
Pensions	8 825	9 289	9 657	9 848	10 316	10 345	10 589	11 146	11 411	11 406	11 282
Unemployment comp.	779	653	609	1 911	3 153	3 167	3 955	4 635	5 015	5 774	7 056
Other social exp.[1]	8 135	9 185	9 624	10 321	10 772	11 019	11 332	12 296	12 932	:	:
Total social exp.	33 031	35 301	36 030	38 792	40 835	41 348	42 784	45 695	47 839	:	:
Total government exp.	50 992	53 216	53 542	58 302	58 734	59 851	61 621	65 624	76 433	:	:
GDP	121 531	128 149	133 061	132 089	130 771	139 331	142 541	145 062	150 404	149 730	148 674
PRICE INDEXES (1970 = 1.0000)											
Education	:	:	:	:	:	:	:	:	:	:	:
Health	1.1050	1.1952	1.2598	1.4660	1.6946	1.7945	1.8991	2.0637	2.1763	2.4112	2.7077
Private consumption	1.0816	1.1704	1.2965	1.4851	1.6339	1.7942	1.9656	2.1426	2.3653	2.6367	2.9547
Government consumption	1.1160	1.2148	1.3406	1.5923	1.8343	1.9982	2.1527	2.3149	2.4904	2.7471	3.0546
Gross Domestic Product	1.0789	1.1762	1.2991	1.4659	1.6537	1.8030	1.9595	2.1465	2.3064	2.4964	2.7616

FINLAND (In millions of Markkaa)

	1960	1961	1962	1963	1964	1965	1966	1967	1968	1969	1970
AT CURRENT PRICES :											
Education[1]	1 053	1 162	1 283	1 417	1 564	1 726	1 906	2 105	2 324	2 565	2 832
Health	364	413	443	518	630	824	946	1 191	1 423	1 631	1 839
Pensions	532	613	712	780	914	1 058	1 315	1 471	1 856	2 101	2 483
Unemployment comp.	1	4	6	12	17	22	39	66	133	133	95
Other social exp.	516	620	705	751	874	1 011	1 090	1 233	1 386	1 521	1 665
Total social exp.	2 466	2 812	3 149	3 478	3 999	4 641	5 296	6 066	7 122	7 951	8 914
Total government exp.	4 235	4 668	5 281	6 087	7 188	8 140	9 084	10 220	11 737	12 802	13 954
GDP	16 038	18 141	19 392	21 026	23 718	26 216	28 071	30 744	35 231	40 228	44 858
AT 1970 PRICES :											
Education[1]	2 197	2 293	2 395	2 429	2 406	2 485	2 549	2 589	2 571	2 707	2 832
Health	531	578	631	728	809	1 016	1 121	1 372	1 476	1 646	1 839
Pensions	860	963	1 074	1 119	1 212	1 341	1 611	1 692	1 958	2 163	2 483
Unemployment comp.	2	6	9	17	23	28	48	76	140	95	95
Other social exp.	834	974	1 063	1 077	1 159	1 282	1 335	1 418	1 462	1 566	1 665
Total social exp.	4 424	4 814	5 172	5 370	5 609	6 152	6 664	7 147	7 607	8 219	8 914
Total government exp.	8 116	8 476	9 152	9 842	10 514	11 189	11 730	12 256	12 713	13 339	13 954
GDP	27 990	30 110	30 918	31 940	33 628	35 408	36 151	36 987	37 919	41 571	44 858
PRICE INDEXES (1970 = 1.0000)											
Education	0.6855	0.7141	0.7020	0.7119	0.7787	0.8113	0.8438	0.8681	0.9638	0.9908	1.0000
Health	0.6185	0.6363	0.6630	0.6973	0.7540	0.7888	0.8162	0.8693	0.9477	0.9713	1.0000
Private consumption	0.4792	0.5068	0.5357	0.5834	0.6501	0.6946	0.7477	0.8130	0.9038	0.9475	1.0000
Government consumption											
Gross Domestic Product	0.5730	0.6025	0.6272	0.6583	0.7053	0.7404	0.7765	0.8312	0.9291	0.9677	1.0000

	1971	1972	1973	1974	1975	1976	1977	1978	1979	1980	1981
AT CURRENT PRICES :											
Education[1]	3 331	3 838	4 534	5 891	6 765	8 064	8 978	9 026	10 126	11 515	13 269
Health	2 063	2 588	3 057	3 880	5 031	6 078	6 795	7 283	8 086	9 440	10 953
Pensions	3 038	3 644	4 452	5 988	7 475	9 370	11 271	12 667	14 018	16 151	18 657
Unemployment comp.	117	196	169	172	224	473	856	1 245	1 131	993	1 242
Other social exp.	1 891	2 264	2 633	3 263	4 284	5 289	6 439	7 171	8 001	9 277	10 871
Total social exp.	10 440	12 530	14 845	19 194	23 779	29 274	34 339	37 392	41 362	47 376	54 992
Total government exp.	16 071	19 049	22 189	28 895	37 294	43 858	49 989	54 590	62 026	71 332	82 641
GDP	49 243	57 401	69 845	88 143	101 882	115 003	127 065	139 918	161 957	186 846	211 946
AT 1970 PRICES :											
Education[1]	3 058	3 237	3 390	3 607	3 402	3 578	3 685	3 512	3 604	3 666	3 757
Health	1 985	2 333	2 390	2 635	2 861	3 087	3 165	3 117	3 233	3 438	3 609
Pensions	2 855	3 152	3 427	3 885	4 167	4 624	4 979	5 197	5 336	5 552	5 757
Unemployment comp.	110	170	130	112	125	233	378	511	431	341	383
Other social exp.	1 777	1 958	2 027	2 117	2 388	2 610	2 844	2 942	3 046	3 189	3 354
Total social exp.	9 785	10 850	11 364	12 356	12 943	14 132	15 051	15 279	15 650	16 186	16 860
Total government exp.	14 954	16 348	16 855	18 295	19 739	20 603	21 474	21 971	23 005	23 813	24 688
GDP	45 684	49 128	53 996	53 996	54 311	54 450	54 647	55 891	60 138	63 770	64 750
PRICE INDEXES (1970 = 1.0000)											
Education	1.0392	1.1093	1.2790	1.4724	1.7582	1.9690	2.1469	2.3364	2.5014	2.7460	3.0345
Health	1.0640	1.1560	1.2992	1.5414	1.7937	2.0264	2.2637	2.4374	2.6269	2.9088	3.2408
Private consumption	1.0894	1.1858	1.3375	1.6334	1.9886	2.2536	2.4366	2.5701	2.8097	3.1411	3.5319
Government consumption											
Gross Domestic Product	1.0779	1.1684	1.3345	1.6324	1.8759	2.1121	2.3252	2.5034	2.6931	2.9300	3.2733

GREECE (In billions of Drachmae)

	1960	1961	1962	1963	1964	1965	1966	1967	1968	1969	1970
AT CURRENT PRICES:											
Education[1]	1.7	1.9	2.0	2.3	2.9	3.4	3.8	4.3	4.6	5.0	5.6
Health	1.8	2.1	2.4	2.7	3.3	4.0	4.6	4.8	5.0	5.7	6.4
Pensions	..	..	4.8	5.9	6.6	7.7	9.3	11.2	12.8	14.0	16.0
Unemployment comp.	..	..	0.3	0.4	0.5	0.5	0.5	0.9	0.6	0.6	0.6
Other social exp.[2]	5.4	6.1	1.4	1.5	1.8	2.5	2.7	2.9	3.6	3.9	4.0
Total social exp.	8.9	10.1	10.9	12.7	15.0	18.1	20.9	24.1	26.8	29.2	32.6
Total government exp.	24.6	28.0	31.2	33.8	39.6	46.5	53.5	63.1	68.4	76.5	84.1
GDP	105.2	118.6	126.0	140.7	158.0	179.8	200.0	216.1	234.5	266.5	298.9
AT 1970 PRICES:											
Education[1]	2.8	3.0	3.2	3.5	4.1	4.5	4.9	5.0	5.0	5.3	5.6
Health	2.9	3.3	3.7	4.0	4.7	5.4	5.9	5.6	5.5	6.0	6.4
Pensions	..	..	6.0	7.1	7.8	8.7	10.1	12.0	13.6	14.4	16.0
Unemployment comp.	..	..	0.4	0.5	0.6	0.5	0.6	1.0	0.9	0.7	0.6
Other social exp.[2]	7.0	7.8	1.8	1.8	2.1	2.8	3.0	3.1	3.8	4.0	4.0
Total social exp.	12.7	14.0	15.0	16.8	19.2	22.0	24.4	26.6	28.8	30.3	32.6
Total government exp.	38.9	42.8	46.7	48.4	54.0	60.2	65.9	71.9	74.4	80.1	84.1
GDP	143.4	159.4	161.8	178.2	192.9	211.1	223.9	236.2	251.9	276.9	298.9
PRICE INDEXES (1970 = 1.0000)											
Education	..	..	..	..	..	..	..	..	..	..	..
Health	..	..	..	..	..	..	..	..	..	..	..
Private consumption	0.7831	0.7917	0.8018	0.8287	0.8472	0.8858	0.9165	0.9342	0.9412	0.9696	1.0000
Government consumption	0.6003	0.6254	0.6395	0.6660	0.7078	0.7438	0.7845	0.8613	0.9131	0.9504	1.0000
Gross Domestic Product	0.7334	0.7444	0.7787	0.7896	0.8189	0.8517	0.8931	0.9149	0.9308	0.9623	1.0000

	1971	1972	1973	1974	1975	1976	1977	1978	1979	1980	1981
AT CURRENT PRICES:											
Education[1]	6.3	6.8	8.4	10.7	13.0	16.4	21.4	27.7	33.1	40.7	..
Health	7.5	8.6	10.5	13.3	16.4	22.4	29.2	36.4	45.4	60.2	81.1
Pensions	17.3	18.3	21.4	25.8	32.0	39.7	50.6	67.6	77.8	97.7	..
Unemployment comp.	0.5	0.5	0.5	1.4	2.4	1.9	2.8	3.7	4.5	5.3	9.0
Other social exp.[2]	4.7	5.3	5.8	6.6	7.3	10.6	13.3	16.1	21.5	26.0	..
Total social exp.	36.3	39.6	46.5	57.9	71.2	91.1	117.3	151.5	182.3	229.9	..
Total government exp.	97.9	111.3	135.1	171.9	209.1	259.6	315.0	389.3	477.1	575.0	..
GDP	330.3	377.7	484.2	564.2	672.2	824.9	963.7	1 161.4	1 428.8	1 710.1	2 043.2
AT 1970 PRICES:											
Education[1]	6.0	6.2	6.8	6.9	7.1	7.8	8.7	9.7	9.8	10.1	..
Health	7.2	7.8	8.4	8.6	9.0	10.6	11.9	12.8	13.4	14.9	16.3
Pensions	16.8	17.2	17.5	17.1	18.8	20.5	23.4	27.8	27.3	28.1	..
Unemployment comp.	0.5	0.5	0.4	0.4	1.4	1.0	1.3	1.5	1.6	1.5	2.1
Other social exp.[2]	4.6	5.0	4.7	4.4	4.3	5.5	6.1	6.6	7.5	7.5	..
Total social exp.	35.1	36.8	37.9	37.8	40.7	45.4	51.5	58.4	59.5	62.1	..
Total government exp.	94.1	102.1	109.2	111.0	116.5	125.4	132.2	141.9	146.4	147.4	..
GDP	320.2	348.6	374.2	360.5	382.4	406.7	420.6	448.8	465.3	473.0	471.1
PRICE INDEXES (1970 = 1.0000)											
Education	..	..	..	..	..	..	..	..	..	..	..
Health	1.0110	1.0855	1.2885	1.5891	1.9211	2.3491	2.6099	3.0201	3.3974	3.9765	4.3064
Private consumption	1.0286	1.0625	1.2216	1.5094	1.7029	1.9324	2.1631	2.4323	2.8516	3.4763	..
Government consumption	1.0443	1.0978	1.2404	1.5584	1.8191	2.1090	2.4497	2.8485	3.3943	4.0442	4.9697
Gross Domestic Product	1.0315	1.0835	1.2940	1.5649	1.7579	2.0285	2.2912	2.5878	3.0703	3.6154	4.3370

IRELAND (In millions of Irish Pounds)

	1960	1961	1962	1963	1964	1965	1966	1967	1968	1969	1970
AT CURRENT PRICES :											
Education[1]	18.7	21.7	25.2	29.3	36.7	41.2	42.3	49.7	61.7	72.8	83.8
Health	19.0	20.0	23.0	25.0	28.0	32.1	37.1	44.0	45.5	56.2	70.0
Pensions	15.9	18.7	19.7	21.6	23.8	26.7	30.1	31.8	35.8	41.5	51.1
Unemployment comp.	3.8	4.1	4.7	5.5	5.9	6.7	8.7	10.4	13.1	15.8	20.8
Other social exp.[1]	16.2	17.2	18.4	21.8	25.3	26.5	29.2	31.3	34.9	43.4	50.7
Total social exp.	73.6	81.7	91.0	103.2	119.7	133.2	147.4	167.2	191.0	229.7	276.4
Total government exp.[2]	202.0	221.6	248.0	275.4	324.2	346.2	366.8	405.0	462.0	539.4	613.6
GDP	631.3	679.7	735.8	791.3	900.6	958.9	1 010.4	1 103.6	1 245.2	1 438.3	1 620.2
AT 1970 PRICES :											
Education[1]	37.4	41.6	45.5	50.7	54.6	58.5	57.7	66.5	76.5	82.6	83.8
Health	38.0	38.3	41.5	43.3	41.7	45.6	50.6	58.8	56.4	63.7	70.0
Pensions	25.5	29.2	29.5	31.6	32.6	34.9	37.9	38.8	41.6	44.9	51.1
Unemployment comp.	6.1	6.4	7.6	8.0	8.1	8.8	11.0	12.7	15.2	17.1	20.8
Other social exp.[1]	25.9	26.8	27.6	31.9	34.6	34.6	36.8	38.2	40.5	46.9	50.7
Total social exp.	132.9	142.3	151.1	165.5	171.6	182.4	194.0	215.0	230.2	255.2	276.4
Total government exp.[2]	389.9	410.3	434.6	463.4	475.9	484.8	493.4	533.0	566.0	606.5	613.6
GDP	1 063.2	1 113.5	1 154.6	1 210.3	1 261.0	1 286.1	1 298.9	1 365.7	1 476.6	1 565.9	1 620.2
PRICE INDEXES (1970 = 1.0000)											
Education	:	:	:	:	:	:	:	:	:	:	:
Health	:	:	:	:	:	:	:	:	:	:	1.0000
Private consumption	0.6246	0.6410	0.6667	0.6833	0.7307	0.7655	0.7943	0.8188	0.8616	0.9253	1.0000
Government consumption	0.4996	0.5221	0.5537	0.5780	0.6720	0.7044	0.7327	0.7478	0.8070	0.8817	1.0000
Gross Domestic Product	0.5938	0.6104	0.6373	0.6538	0.7142	0.7456	0.7779	0.8081	0.8433	0.9185	1.0000

	1971	1972	1973	1974	1975	1976	1977	1978	1979	1980	1981
AT CURRENT PRICES :											
Education[1]	96.4	117.3	144.9	170.4	225.7	272.0	321.4	382.4	467.0	572.4	734.8
Health	88.4	112.5	144.3	178.4	240.2	291.3	347.1	431.0	543.0	744.0	868.0
Pensions	63.3	72.4	94.4	114.4	158.5	193.3	223.3	263.1	308.9	418.1	538.8
Unemployment comp.	24.6	30.4	36.0	46.4	86.2	110.8	116.5	122.8	123.4	176.5	258.8
Other social exp.[1]	56.2	61.8	89.1	114.2	150.8	179.5	212.4	236.3	286.9	363.0	542.6
Total social exp.	328.9	394.4	508.7	623.8	861.4	1 046.9	1 220.7	1 435.6	1 729.2	2 274.0	2 943.0
Total government exp.[2]	715.5	841.8	1 031.4	1 259.9	1 734.4	2 092.0	2 451.5	2 934.7	3 387.8	4 346.0	5 460.0
GDP	1 853.1	2 237.5	2 701.0	2 987.5	3 728.0	4 581.8	5 502.7	6 422.3	7 466.2	8 866.0	10 575.0
AT 1970 PRICES :											
Education[1]	88.0	94.8	101.4	105.7	108.5	112.8	117.3	125.9	132.9	133.6	141.1
Health	80.7	90.9	101.0	110.7	115.5	120.8	126.7	141.9	154.5	173.6	166.7
Pensions	57.8	60.3	70.5	73.8	83.6	85.8	87.8	96.1	98.5	113.8	122.6
Unemployment comp.	22.5	25.3	26.9	30.0	45.5	49.2	44.9	44.9	39.5	48.0	58.9
Other social exp.[1]	51.4	51.5	66.6	73.7	79.6	79.7	83.6	86.3	91.8	98.8	123.5
Total social exp.	300.3	322.8	366.4	393.9	432.7	448.3	461.2	495.1	517.5	567.8	612.8
Total government exp.[2]	653.2	684.4	732.2	788.5	852.5	881.7	910.4	988.6	989.5	1 051.4	1 096.1
GDP	1 676.0	1 782.9	1 867.1	1 946.6	1 985.9	2 029.0	2 166.7	2 293.0	2 370.8	2 459.4	2 498.9
PRICE INDEXES (1970 = 1.0000)											
Education	:	:	:	:	:	:	:	:	:	:	:
Health	1.2378	1.3366	1.4393	1.5308	1.8182	2.1824	2.5527	2.8875	3.1479	:	:
Private consumption	1.0944	1.2001	1.3388	1.5491	1.8953	2.2526	2.5420	2.7369	3.1257	3.6755	4.3950
Government consumption	1.0957	1.2373	1.4288	1.6119	2.0796	2.4116	2.7397	3.0379	3.5139	4.2848	5.2083
Gross Domestic Product	1.1057	1.2550	1.4466	1.5347	1.8772	2.2582	2.5397	2.8008	3.1492	3.6050	4.2319

NETHERLANDS (In millions of Guilders)

	1960	1961	1962	1963	1964	1965	1966	1967	1968	1969	1970
AT CURRENT PRICES :											
Education	1 993	2 228	2 541	2 845	3 626	4 183	4 804	5 501	6 196	7 204	8 028
Health	576	782	1 061	1 440	1 766	2 166	2 656	3 257	3 944	4 941	6 113
Pensions	2 298	2 439	2 782	3 581	4 344	5 501	6 431	7 340	7 780	9 129	10 506
Unemployment comp.	103	77	139	308	171	190	284	358	334	330	437
Other social exp.	2 172	2 593	2 795	3 146	3 777	4 349	5 023	5 889	7 291	8 604	9 997
Total social exp.	7 142	8 119	9 318	11 320	13 684	16 389	19 198	22 345	25 565	30 208	35 081
Total government exp.	13 179	14 677	15 974	18 512	21 982	25 105	28 541	32 688	36 711	42 081	48 943
GDP	44 004	46 458	50 013	54 260	63 848	71 309	77 647	85 186	94 456	106 976	120 499
AT 1970 PRICES :											
Education	4 894	5 124	5 391	5 516	6 008	6 323	6 623	6 911	7 342	7 822	8 028
Health	1 415	1 799	2 251	2 792	2 926	3 074	3 662	4 092	4 674	5 365	6 113
Pensions	3 430	3 555	3 952	4 902	5 569	6 782	7 521	8 336	8 616	9 532	10 506
Unemployment comp.	154	112	197	422	219	234	332	407	370	345	437
Other social exp.	3 242	3 779	3 970	4 307	4 842	5 362	5 874	6 688	8 074	8 984	9 997
Total social exp.	13 135	14 369	15 761	17 939	19 564	21 975	24 012	26 434	29 076	32 048	35 081
Total government exp.	27 961	29 452	29 884	31 882	33 314	35 149	36 894	39 428	42 307	44 939	48 943
GDP	72 842	75 078	78 060	80 888	87 583	92 178	94 715	99 714	106 106	112 927	120 499
PRICE INDEXES (1970 = 1.0000)											
Education	..	..	..	..	..	..	..	..	..	0.9058	1.0000
Health	..	..	..	..	..	..	..	..	..	..	..
Private consumption	0.6700	0.6861	0.7040	0.7305	0.7800	0.8111	0.8551	0.8805	0.9030	0.9577	1.0000
Government consumption	0.4072	0.4348	0.4713	0.5158	0.6035	0.6616	0.7253	0.7960	0.8439	0.9210	1.0000
Gross Domestic Product	0.6041	0.6188	0.6407	0.6708	0.7290	0.7736	0.8198	0.8543	0.8902	0.9473	1.0000

	1971	1972	1973	1974	1975	1976	1977	1978	1979	1980	1981
AT CURRENT PRICES :											
Education	9 310	10 550	11 870	14 060	16 630	18 550	20 340	22 020	23 460	24 210	24 760
Health	6 688	7 658	9 029	10 798	12 974	14 755	16 426	18 265	19 831	21 761	23 481
Pensions	12 420	14 420	16 640	19 490	23 480	27 690	32 270	36 760	39 850	43 120	45 580
Unemployment comp.	480	770	680	990	1 560	1 570	1 280	1 350	2 380	2 070	3 460
Other social exp.	12 280	14 690	17 920	22 170	27 090	30 770	20 260	22 650	24 760	28 230	29 390
Total social exp.	41 178	48 088	56 139	67 508	81 734	93 335	90 576	101 045	110 281	119 391	126 671
Total government exp.	57 990	66 810	77 540	91 250	111 040	127 640	143 980	159 550	174 140	191 180	206 590
GDP	136 355	154 319	176 805	200 132	220 251	252 591	274 930	297 010	315 960	335 850	350 540
AT 1970 PRICES :											
Education	8 304	8 488	8 569	8 761	9 147	9 353	9 632	9 856	9 928	9 793	9 739
Health	5 965	6 161	6 518	6 728	7 136	7 439	7 778	8 176	8 392	8 802	9 236
Pensions	11 463	12 232	12 919	13 748	14 956	16 205	17 814	19 423	20 165	20 411	20 266
Unemployment comp.	443	653	528	698	994	919	707	713	1 204	980	1 538
Other social exp.	11 334	12 461	13 913	15 638	17 256	18 008	11 184	11 968	12 529	13 363	13 067
Total social exp.	37 509	39 995	42 447	45 573	49 489	51 924	47 115	50 136	52 218	53 349	53 846
Total government exp.	52 504	55 058	57 897	60 366	65 608	69 220	72 403	76 323	79 241	82 388	85 280
GDP	125 650	129 942	137 356	142 210	140 744	148 234	151 752	155 478	159 166	160 112	157 972
PRICE INDEXES (1970 = 1.0000)											
Education	1.1404	1.3450	1.5197	1.7502	2.0649	2.2872	2.4976	2.6922	2.8549	..	..
Health	..	..	..	..	..	..	..	..	..	..	..
Private consumption	1.0835	1.1789	1.2880	1.4177	1.5699	1.7087	1.8115	1.8926	1.9762	2.1126	2.2491
Government consumption	1.1212	1.2429	1.3852	1.6049	1.8181	1.9834	2.1118	2.2341	2.3631	2.4722	2.5424
Gross Domestic Product	1.0852	1.1876	1.2872	1.4073	1.5649	1.7040	1.8117	1.9103	1.9851	2.0976	2.2190

NEW ZEALAND (In millions of New Zealand Dollars)

	1960	1961	1962	1963	1964	1965	1966	1967	1968	1969	1970
AT CURRENT PRICES :											
Education[1]	75.0	85.0	89.7	98.4	109.0	126.0	138.4	156.6	169.3	176.5	202.3
Health	92.0	100.4	106.4	115.8	122.6	135.1	149.6	163.7	170.1	180.7	201.7
Pensions	123.6	110.9	138.7	135.9	152.7	157.2	170.2	179.7	188.1	205.9	231.6
Unemployment comp.	0.2	0.2	0.2	0.3	0.2	0.1	0.1	2.2	3.3	1.5	1.0
Other social exp.[1]	75.8	83.8	82.1	87.8	88.7	92.4	89.9	96.2	96.3	101.7	103.4
Total social exp.	366.6	380.3	417.2	438.2	473.2	510.8	548.2	598.4	627.1	666.3	740.0
Total government exp.	836.5	890.7	925.7	978.9	1 056.4	1 140.6	1 249.8	1 348.9	1 387.6	1 461.5	1 586.1
GDP	2 813.0	2 872.0	3 114.0	3 397.0	3 721.0	4 012.0	4 190.0	4 375.0	4 642.0	5 133.0	5 832.0
AT 1970 PRICES :											
Education[1]	138.2	149.5	149.9	161.9	167.4	172.7	180.8	203.4	208.6	203.2	202.3
Health	169.6	176.6	177.8	190.5	188.3	185.1	195.4	212.6	209.6	208.0	201.7
Pensions	171.5	152.9	188.5	182.6	198.1	198.6	209.6	204.8	208.1	220.1	231.6
Unemployment comp.	0.3	0.3	0.4	0.4	0.3	0.1	0.1	2.5	3.7	1.6	1.6
Other social exp.[1]	105.2	115.5	111.6	117.9	115.1	116.7	110.7	109.6	106.6	108.7	103.4
Total social exp.	584.8	594.8	628.2	653.3	669.2	673.2	696.6	732.9	736.6	741.6	740.0
Total government exp.	1 451.0	1 492.4	1 478.0	1 542.8	1 565.1	1 536.2	1 613.1	1 707.4	1 673.6	1 657.0	1 586.1
GDP	4 167.4	4 221.0	4 427.1	4 639.4	4 885.8	5 082.3	5 257.9	5 225.1	5 295.5	5 718.6	5 832.0
PRICE INDEXES (1970 = 1.0000)											
Education	...										
Health	...										
Private consumption	0.7208	0.7255	0.7357	0.7444	0.7709	0.7916	0.8120	0.8776	0.9037	0.9356	1.0000
Government consumption	0.5425	0.5686	0.5984	0.6079	0.6510	0.7298	0.7655	0.7701	0.8116	0.8687	1.0000
Gross Domestic Product	0.6750	0.6804	0.7034	0.7322	0.7616	0.7894	0.7969	0.8373	0.8766	0.8976	1.0000

	1971	1972	1973	1974	1975	1976	1977	1978	1979	1980	1981
AT CURRENT PRICES :											
Education[1]	259.3	330.0	370.3	432.4	519.4	621.0	690.5	795.5	912.1	1 009.3	1 292.0
Health	240.9	287.7	338.8	404.1	500.5	619.1	706.0	828.0	1 003.0	1 160.0	1 386.0
Pensions	263.3	318.5	384.6	456.2	584.2	734.6	1 069.1	1 317.5	1 504.1	1 743.0	2 098.8
Unemployment comp.	2.7	5.0	3.5	5.2	8.5	13.4	19.9	54.2	66.1	118.8	156.4
Other social exp.[1]	114.7	180.7	233.6	243.9	260.0	306.7	383.6	406.5	511.7	649.3	714.9
Total social exp.	880.9	1 121.9	1 330.8	1 541.8	1 872.6	2 294.8	2 869.1	3 401.7	3 997.0	4 680.4	5 648.1
Total government exp.	1 836.0	2 171.0	2 526.1	2 909.0	3 526.7	4 416.4	4 880.1	5 873.0	7 035.1	9 133.4	10 973.7
GDP	6 863.0	7 892.0	9 135.0	10 028.0	11 484.0	13 792.0	15 217.0	17 541.0	20 966.0	24 127.0	28 598.0
AT 1970 PRICES :											
Education[1]	229.1	286.7	275.4	282.6	296.4	313.2	299.8	297.1	297.2	264.2	280.8
Health	212.8	249.9	251.9	264.1	285.7	312.3	306.5	309.2	326.8	303.7	301.3
Pensions	235.1	269.8	307.5	333.7	370.8	391.7	501.4	563.0	552.6	540.7	577.4
Unemployment comp.	2.4	4.2	2.8	3.8	5.4	7.1	9.3	23.2	24.3	36.9	43.0
Other social exp.[1]	102.4	153.1	186.7	178.4	165.0	163.5	179.9	173.7	188.0	201.4	196.7
Total social exp.	781.8	963.7	1 024.3	1 062.6	1 123.3	1 187.8	1 296.9	1 366.2	1 388.9	1 346.9	1 399.2
Total government exp.	1 625.5	1 875.1	1 913.1	1 956.1	2 067.4	2 257.9	2 170.0	2 289.0	2 378.9	2 512.7	2 556.7
GDP	6 055.8	6 345.6	6 752.2	7 170.5	7 142.7	7 294.3	6 972.9	7 018.9	6 899.4	7 294.2	7 324.9
PRICE INDEXES (1970 = 1.0000)											
Education	...										
Health	...										
Private consumption	1.1200	1.1806	1.2509	1.3669	1.5757	1.8756	2.1323	2.3402	2.7220	3.2235	3.6349
Government consumption	1.1320	1.1511	1.3448	1.5302	1.7521	1.9827	2.3032	2.6780	3.0688	3.8196	4.6008
Gross Domestic Product	1.1333	1.2437	1.3529	1.3985	1.6078	1.8908	2.1823	2.4991	3.0388	3.3077	3.9042

NORWAY (In millions of Kroner)

	1960	1961	1962	1963	1964	1965	1966	1967	1968	1969	1970
AT CURRENT PRICES :											
Education	1 272	1 531	1 904	2 202	2 558	2 867	3 261	3 737	4 070	4 501	5 115
Health[3]	915	1 020	1 132	1 292	1 469	1 612	1 950	2 194	2 435	2 855	3 664
Pensions	936	1 121	1 444	1 575	1 841	2 392	2 992	3 515	4 005	4 725	5 688
Unemployment comp.[2]	51	51	58	76	57	52	52	52	65	82	68
Other social exp.[1]	694	731	795	914	1 008	1 078	1 115	1 367	1 522	1 668	3 465
Total social exp.	3 868	4 454	5 333	6 059	6 933	8 001	9 370	10 861	12 097	13 831	18 000
Total government exp.[3]	8 724	9 524	12 236	13 789	15 160	17 302	18 982	21 719	24 149	27 703	32 743
GDP	33 058	36 062	38 843	41 682	45 837	50 563	54 568	59 700	63 749	69 418	79 877
AT 1970 PRICES :											
Education	2 236	2 628	2 924	3 274	3 646	3 897	4 120	4 532	4 681	4 909	5 115
Health[3]	1 609	1 751	1 738	1 921	2 094	2 191	2 464	2 661	2 801	3 114	3 664
Pensions	1 431	1 666	2 055	2 177	2 431	3 031	3 664	4 118	4 552	5 187	5 688
Unemployment comp.[2]	78	76	83	105	75	66	64	56	74	90	68
Other social exp.[1]	1 061	1 086	1 131	1 263	1 331	1 366	1 366	1 602	1 730	1 831	3 465
Total social exp.	6 415	7 207	7 931	8 740	9 577	10 551	11 678	12 969	13 838	15 131	18 000
Total government exp.[3]	14 952	15 911	18 531	20 234	21 305	23 195	23 822	26 137	27 700	30 262	32 743
GDP	53 003	56 329	57 914	60 104	63 119	66 452	68 969	73 279	74 937	78 315	79 877
PRICE INDEXES (1970 = 1.0000)											
Education	:	:	0.6541	0.6679	0.6962	0.7225	0.7864	0.8212	0.8687	0.9121	1.0000
Health	:	:	0.6102	0.6463	0.6826	0.7211	0.7808	0.8316	0.8792	0.9186	1.0000
Private consumption	0.6540	0.6729	0.7028	0.7235	0.7572	0.7892	0.8165	0.8535	0.8799	0.9110	1.0000
Government consumption	0.5688	0.5825	0.6512	0.6725	0.7015	0.7356	0.7915	0.8246	0.8694	0.9168	1.0000
Gross Domestic Product	0.6237	0.6402	0.6707	0.6935	0.7262	0.7609	0.7912	0.8147	0.8507	0.8864	1.0000

	1971	1972	1973	1974	1975	1976	1977	1978	1979	1980	1981
AT CURRENT PRICES :											
Education	6 134	6 687	7 391	8 400	10 027	11 696	13 297	15 048	15 911	17 816	20 060
Health[3]	4 285	5 562	6 477	7 573	9 591	11 385	13 362	15 172	16 708	18 623	21 072
Pensions	6 713	7 532	8 817	10 155	11 811	13 817	16 164	18 485	19 855	22 485	25 905
Unemployment comp.[2]	89	116	106	171	171	297	247	340	489	646	358
Other social exp.[1]	4 421	5 156	5 939	6 297	7 421	9 042	9 923	12 371	15 554	18 084	20 864
Total social exp.	21 642	25 053	28 730	32 596	39 021	46 237	52 993	61 416	68 517	77 654	88 796
Total government exp.[3]	38 349	43 934	49 909	57 889	69 272	82 850	96 022	111 415	121 563	139 181	157 832
GDP	89 107	98 403	111 853	129 729	148 701	170 709	191 534	213 079	238 668	285 045	328 551
AT 1970 PRICES :											
Education	5 509	5 616	5 734	5 817	6 117	6 452	6 792	7 183	7 351	7 513	7 570
Health[3]	3 848	4 671	5 025	5 244	5 851	6 280	6 825	7 242	7 719	7 854	7 952
Pensions	6 309	6 643	7 214	7 609	7 924	8 528	9 187	9 704	9 914	10 220	10 362
Unemployment comp.[2]	84	102	87	128	115	183	140	178	244	294	358
Other social exp.[1]	4 155	4 547	4 859	4 718	4 979	5 581	5 640	6 495	7 766	8 219	8 346
Total social exp.	19 905	21 579	22 919	23 516	24 986	27 024	28 584	30 802	32 994	34 100	34 588
Total government exp.[3]	34 909	37 436	39 350	41 032	43 442	47 220	50 563	54 668	57 501	60 048	60 641
GDP	83 535	87 852	91 465	96 217	100 223	107 048	110 880	115 917	121 788	127 076	127 429
PRICE INDEXES (1970 = 1.0000)											
Education	1.1239	1.2052	1.3042	1.4533	1.6539	1.8343	1.9497	1.9048	2.0028	2.2002	2.5000
Health	1.1214	1.2069	1.3055	1.4416	1.6573	4.8905	3.4076	:	:	:	:
Private consumption	1.0641	1.1339	1.2222	1.3346	1.4906	1.6201	1.7594	2.0950	2.1645	2.3712	2.6498
Government consumption	1.1135	1.1907	1.2890	1.4440	1.6391	1.8129	1.9577	:	:	:	:
Gross Domestic Product	1.0667	1.1201	1.2229	1.3483	1.4837	1.5947	1.7274	1.8382	1.9597	2.2431	2.5783

95

SWEDEN (In millions of Kronor)

	1960	1961	1962	1963	1964	1965	1966	1967	1968	1969	1970
AT CURRENT PRICES :											
Education[1]	3 315	3 727	4 189	4 708	5 299	6 064	6 897	8 010	8 643	9 188	10 701
Health	2 467	2 745	3 051	3 734	4 314	5 032	6 047	7 025	8 201	9 016	10 682
Pensions	3 209	3 563	3 992	4 651	5 082	5 757	6 673	7 586	8 436	9 350	10 762
Unemployment comp.	121	99	114	119	106	134	164	299	368	349	462
Other social exp.[2]	2 015	2 050	2 307	2 819	3 234	3 850	4 248	5 237	5 936	6 463	6 956
Total social exp.	11 127	12 184	13 653	16 031	18 035	20 837	24 029	28 157	31 584	34 366	39 563
Total government exp.	22 570	24 543	27 746	31 896	35 844	40 641	46 728	53 252	60 244	66 037	74 801
GDP	72 160	78 522	85 196	91 359	101 893	112 112	121 957	132 376	140 472	152 555	172 226
AT 1970 PRICES :											
Education[1]	6 134	6 536	6 851	7 564	7 907	8 343	8 653	9 376	9 678	9 868	10 701
Health	3 393	3 692	3 896	4 459	4 987	5 653	6 270	6 840	8 056	8 873	10 682
Pensions	4 679	5 080	5 473	6 302	6 648	7 144	7 769	8 380	9 155	9 816	10 762
Unemployment comp.	176	141	156	161	139	166	191	330	399	366	462
Other social exp.[2]	2 938	2 923	3 163	3 820	4 231	4 777	4 946	5 785	6 442	6 785	6 956
Total social exp.	17 320	18 372	19 539	22 306	23 912	26 083	27 829	30 711	33 730	35 708	39 563
Total government exp.	38 495	40 047	42 589	47 796	50 485	53 331	56 306	60 086	65 820	69 723	74 801
GDP	108 724	114 933	119 876	126 117	134 708	139 860	142 790	147 593	152 970	160 618	172 226
PRICE INDEXES (1970 = 1.0000)											
Education	0.5404	0.5702	0.6114	0.6224	0.6702	0.7268	0.7971	0.8543	0.8931	0.9311	1.0000
Health	0.7270	0.7435	0.7832	0.8374	0.8651	0.8902	0.9644	1.0271	1.0180	1.0161	1.0000
Private consumption	0.6858	0.7014	0.7294	0.7380	0.7644	0.8059	0.8589	0.9053	0.9215	0.9525	1.0000
Government consumption				0.6320	0.6829	0.7516	0.8328	0.9198	0.9262	0.9423	1.0000
Gross Domestic Product	0.6637	0.6832	0.7107	0.7244	0.7564	0.8016	0.8541	0.8969	0.9183	0.9498	1.0000

	1971	1972	1973	1974	1975	1976	1977	1978	1979	1980	1981
AT CURRENT PRICES :											
Education[1]	11 480	12 385	13 165	14 540	16 940	19 569	23 317	26 019	30 127	34 330	37 430
Health	12 249	13 383	14 509	17 582	21 652	25 452	31 014	34 915	38 565	46 074	50 431
Pensions	12 662	14 274	16 399	19 952	24 586	29 485	36 564	42 675	48 606	57 957	66 889
Unemployment comp.	668	669	638	807	730	881	1 193	1 799	1 966	2 044	2 995
Other social exp.[2]	8 615	9 122	10 179	15 575	16 665	19 485	21 849	24 522	27 075	30 111	32 332
Total social exp.	45 674	49 833	54 890	68 456	80 573	94 872	113 937	129 930	146 339	170 516	190 077
Total government exp.	84 474	93 995	101 521	123 259	147 296	175 605	208 430	241 256	274 050	320 565	366 587
GDP	186 215	203 758	226 744	256 112	300 785	340 197	370 016	412 450	462 307	525 099	571 429
AT 1970 PRICES :											
Education[1]	10 356	10 333	10 161	10 001	10 160	10 282	10 506	10 667	11 394	11 474	11 529
Health	11 480	11 362	11 413	16 016	16 818	17 223	19 185	19 554	20 028	21 178	20 530
Pensions	11 710	12 385	13 238	14 719	16 346	17 677	19 808	20 776	22 048	23 563	24 373
Unemployment comp.	618	580	515	595	485	528	646	876	892	831	1 091
Other social exp.[2]	7 967	7 915	8 217	11 490	11 080	11 682	11 837	11 938	12 281	12 242	11 781
Total social exp.	42 131	42 575	43 544	52 821	54 889	57 392	61 982	63 811	66 643	69 288	69 304
Total government exp.	77 133	79 420	79 536	90 517	94 905	99 812	105 722	109 453	114 945	119 436	123 672
GDP	173 854	177 830	184 886	190 798	195 671	197 743	194 581	197 998	205 598	209 028	207 883
PRICE INDEXES (1970 = 1.0000)											
Education	1.1085	1.1986	1.2956	1.4538	1.6674	1.9032	2.2195	2.4391	2.6440	2.9921	3.2466
Health	1.0670	1.1779	1.2713	1.0978	1.2874	1.4778	1.6166	1.7856	1.9256	2.1756	2.4564
Private consumption	1.0813	1.1525	1.2388	1.3555	1.5041	1.6680	1.8459	2.0541	2.2046	2.4597	2.7444
Government consumption	1.1126	1.1685	1.2237	1.3656	1.5391	1.7440	2.0521	2.2487	2.4822	2.7256	2.9642
Gross Domestic Product	1.0711	1.1458	1.2264	1.3424	1.5372	1.7204	1.9016	2.0831	2.2486	2.5121	2.7488

SWITZERLAND (In millions of Francs)

	1960	1961	1962	1963	1964	1965	1966	1967	1968	1969	1970
AT CURRENT PRICES :											
Education	1 159	1 188	1 363	1 640	1 920	2 099	2 388	2 622	2 912	3 239	3 756
Health[1]	934	1 009	1 144	1 177	1 358	1 592	1 874	2 103	2 357	2 627	2 924
Pensions	858	1 097	1 254	1 323	1 961	2 061	2 162	2 481	2 610	3 810	3 988
Unemployment comp.	9	5	4	6	2	2	2	2	3	2	1
Other social exp.	37	40	348	410	435	504	582	621	652	704	783
Total social exp.	2 997	3 339	4 113	4 556	5 676	6 258	7 008	7 829	8 534	10 382	11 452
Total government exp.	:	:	:	:	:	:	:	:	15 535	17 785	19 300
GDP	37 370	42 040	46 620	51 265	56 825	60 860	65 355	70 350	75 120	81 395	90 665
AT 1970 PRICES :											
Education	1 902	1 861	1 990	2 273	2 486	2 642	2 874	3 017	3 229	3 432	3 756
Health[1]	1 533	1 581	1 671	1 632	1 758	2 004	2 255	2 420	2 614	2 783	2 924
Pensions	1 245	1 548	1 687	1 718	2 443	2 469	2 474	2 720	2 789	3 961	3 988
Unemployment comp.	13	7	5	8	2	2	2	2	3	2	1
Other social exp.	54	56	468	532	542	604	666	681	697	732	783
Total social exp.	4 747	5 053	5 821	6 163	7 231	7 721	8 271	8 840	9 332	10 910	11 452
Total government exp.	:	:	:	:	:	:	:	:	17 096	18 754	19 300
GDP	57 167	61 796	64 759	67 919	71 487	73 761	75 581	77 890	80 687	85 230	90 665
PRICE INDEXES (1970 = 1.0000)											
Education	:	:	:	:	:	:	:	:	:	:	:
Health	:	:	:	:	:	:	:	:	:	:	:
Private consumption	0.6892	0.7086	0.7434	0.7701	0.8028	0.8349	0.8740	0.9123	0.9359	0.9618	1.0000
Government consumption	0.6092	0.6384	0.6848	0.7214	0.7723	0.7946	0.8310	0.8691	0.9017	0.9438	1.0000
Gross Domestic Product	0.6537	0.6803	0.7199	0.7548	0.7949	0.8251	0.8647	0.9032	0.9310	0.9550	1.0000

	1971	1972	1973	1974	1975	1976	1977	1978	1979	1980	1981
AT CURRENT PRICES :											
Education	4 599	5 450	6 522	7 421	7 784	8 192	8 296	8 398	8 721	:	:
Health[1]	3 527	4 144	4 947	5 866	6 765	7 234	7 524	7 962	8 591	:	:
Pensions	4 645	5 191	8 148	9 181	10 730	11 319	12 211	12 506	12 771	13 562	13 799
Unemployment comp.	1	1	1	1	234	564	116	187	189	104	105
Other social exp.	863	959	1 075	1 218	1 292	1 296	1 310	1 379	1 471	1 594	1 712
Total social exp.	13 635	15 745	20 693	23 688	26 805	28 605	29 457	30 432	31 743	:	:
Total government exp.	22 555	25 570	31 435	35 995	40 770	:	:	:	:	:	:
GDP	102 995	116 710	130 060	141 100	140 155	141 960	145 790	151 675	158 545	170 330	185 565
AT 1970 PRICES :											
Education	4 116	4 440	4 729	4 874	4 775	4 887	4 915	4 916	4 904	:	:
Health[1]	3 157	3 376	3 587	3 852	4 150	4 316	4 458	4 661	4 831	:	:
Pensions	4 343	4 510	6 493	6 651	7 290	7 522	8 022	8 167	7 989	8 118	7 749
Unemployment comp.	1	1	1	1	159	375	76	122	118	62	59
Other social exp.	807	833	857	882	878	861	861	901	920	954	961
Total social exp.	12 424	13 160	15 667	16 260	17 252	17 961	18 332	18 767	18 762	:	:
Total government exp.	20 408	21 164	23 456	24 342	25 819	:	:	:	:	:	:
GDP	94 361	97 380	100 347	101 811	94 393	93 070	95 337	95 724	98 110	102 627	104 614
PRICE INDEXES (1970 = 1.0000)											
Education	:	:	:	:	:	:	:	:	:	:	:
Health	:	:	:	:	:	:	:	:	:	:	:
Private consumption	1.0695	1.1509	1.2549	1.3803	1.4718	1.5048	1.5221	1.5313	1.5985	1.6707	1.7808
Government consumption	1.1173	1.2275	1.3792	1.5227	1.6300	1.6762	1.6878	1.7084	1.7782	1.8614	1.9774
Gross Domestic Product	1.0915	1.1985	1.2961	1.3859	1.4848	1.5253	1.5292	1.5845	1.6160	1.6597	1.7738

OECD SALES AGENTS
DÉPOSITAIRES DES PUBLICATIONS DE L'OCDE

ARGENTINA – ARGENTINE
Carlos Hirsch S.R.L., Florida 165, 4° Piso (Galería Guemes)
1333 BUENOS AIRES, Tel. 33.1787.2391 y 30.7122

AUSTRALIA – AUSTRALIE
Australia and New Zealand Book Company Pty, Ltd.,
10 Aquatic Drive, Frenchs Forest, N.S.W. 2086
P.O. Box 459, BROOKVALE, N.S.W. 2100. Tel. (02) 452.44.11

AUSTRIA – AUTRICHE
OECD Publications and Information Center
4 Simrockstrasse 5300 Bonn (Germany). Tel. (0228) 21.60.45
Local Agent/Agent local :
Gerold and Co., Graben 31, WIEN 1. Tel. 52.22.35

BELGIUM – BELGIQUE
Jean De Lannoy, Service Publications OCDE
avenue du Roi 202, B-1060 BRUXELLES. Tel. 02/538.51.69

CANADA
Renouf Publishing Company Limited,
Central Distribution Centre,
61 Sparks Street (Mall),
P.O.B. 1008 - Station B,
OTTAWA, Ont. KIP 5R1.
Tel. (613)238.8985-6
Toll Free: 1-800.267.4164
Librairie Renouf Limitée
980 rue Notre-Dame,
Lachine, P.Q. H8S 2B9,
Tel. (514) 634-7088.

DENMARK – DANEMARK
Munksgaard Export and Subscription Service
35, Nørre Søgade
DK 1370 KØBENHAVN K. Tel. +45.1.12.85.70

FINLAND – FINLANDE
Akateeminen Kirjakauppa
Keskuskatu 1, 00100 HELSINKI 10. Tel. 65.11.22

FRANCE
Bureau des Publications de l'OCDE,
2 rue André-Pascal, 75775 PARIS CEDEX 16. Tel. (1) 524.81.67
Principal correspondant :
13602 AIX-EN-PROVENCE : Librairie de l'Université.
Tel. 26.18.08

GERMANY – ALLEMAGNE
OECD Publications and Information Center
4 Simrockstrasse 5300 BONN Tel. (0228) 21.60.45

GREECE – GRÈCE
Librairie Kauffmann, 28 rue du Stade,
ATHÈNES 132. Tel. 322.21.60

HONG-KONG
Government Information Services,
Publications/Sales Section, Baskerville House,
2nd Floor, 22 Ice House Street

ICELAND – ISLANDE
Snaebjörn Jónsson and Co., h.f.,
Hafnarstraeti 4 and 9, P.O.B. 1131, REYKJAVIK.
Tel. 13133/14281/11936

INDIA – INDE
Oxford Book and Stationery Co. :
NEW DELHI-1, Scindia House. Tel. 45896
CALCUTTA 700016, 17 Park Street. Tel. 240832

INDONESIA – INDONÉSIE
PDIN-LIPI, P.O. Box 3065/JKT., JAKARTA, Tel. 583467

IRELAND – IRLANDE
TDC Publishers – Library Suppliers
12 North Frederick Street, DUBLIN 1 Tel. 744835-749677

ITALY – ITALIE
Libreria Commissionaria Sansoni :
Via Lamarmora 45, 50121 FIRENZE. Tel. 579751/584468
Via Bartolini 29, 20155 MILANO. Tel. 365083
Sub-depositari :
Ugo Tassi
Via A. Farnese 28, 00192 ROMA. Tel. 310590
Editrice e Libreria Herder,
Piazza Montecitorio 120, 00186 ROMA. Tel. 6794628
Costantino Ercolano, Via Generale Orsini 46, 80132 NAPOLI. Tel. 405210
Libreria Hoepli, Via Hoepli 5, 20121 MILANO. Tel. 865446
Libreria Scientifica, Dott. Lucio de Biasio "Aeiou"
Via Meravigli 16, 20123 MILANO Tel. 807679
Libreria Zanichelli
Piazza Galvani 1/A, 40124 Bologna Tel. 237389
Libreria Lattes, Via Garibaldi 3, 10122 TORINO. Tel. 519274
La diffusione delle edizioni OCSE è inoltre assicurata dalle migliori librerie nelle
città più importanti.

JAPAN – JAPON
OECD Publications and Information Center,
Landic Akasaka Bldg., 2-3-4 Akasaka,
Minato-ku, TOKYO 107 Tel. 586.2016

KOREA – CORÉE
Pan Korea Book Corporation,
P.O. Box n° 101 Kwangwhamun, SÉOUL. Tel. 72.7369

LEBANON – LIBAN
Documenta Scientifica/Redico,
Edison Building, Bliss Street, P.O. Box 5641, BEIRUT.
Tel. 354429 – 344425

MALAYSIA – MALAISIE
University of Malaya Co-operative Bookshop Ltd.
P.O. Box 1127, Jalan Pantai Baru
KUALA LUMPUR. Tel. 577701/577072

THE NETHERLANDS – PAYS-BAS
Staatsuitgeverij, Verzendboekhandel,
Chr. Plantijnstraat 1 Postbus 20014
2500 EA S-GRAVENHAGE. Tel. nr. 070.789911
Voor bestellingen: Tel. 070.789208

NEW ZEALAND – NOUVELLE-ZÉLANDE
Publications Section,
Government Printing Office Bookshops:
AUCKLAND: Retail Bookshop: 25 Rutland Street,
Mail Orders: 85 Beach Road, Private Bag C.P.O.
HAMILTON: Retail: Ward Street,
Mail Orders, P.O. Box 857
WELLINGTON: Retail: Mulgrave Street (Head Office),
Cubacade World Trade Centre
Mail Orders: Private Bag
CHRISTCHURCH: Retail: 159 Hereford Street,
Mail Orders: Private Bag
DUNEDIN: Retail: Princes Street
Mail Order: P.O. Box 1104

NORWAY – NORVÈGE
J.G. TANUM A/S
P.O. Box 1177 Sentrum OSLO 1. Tel. (02) 80.12.60

PAKISTAN
Mirza Book Agency, 65 Shahrah Quaid-E-Azam, LAHORE 3.
Tel. 66839

PORTUGAL
Livraria Portugal, Rua do Carmo 70-74,
1117 LISBOA CODEX. Tel. 360582/3

SINGAPORE – SINGAPOUR
Information Publications Pte Ltd,
Pei-Fu Industrial Building,
24 New Industrial Road N° 02-06
SINGAPORE 1953, Tel. 2831786, 2831798

SPAIN – ESPAGNE
Mundi-Prensa Libros, S.A.
Castelló 37, Apartado 1223, MADRID-1. Tel. 275.46.55
Libreria Bosch, Ronda Universidad 11, BARCELONA 7.
Tel. 317.53.08, 317.53.58

SWEDEN – SUÈDE
AB CE Fritzes Kungl Hovbokhandel,
Box 16 356, S 103 27 STH. Regeringsgatan 12,
DS STOCKHOLM. Tel. 08/23.89.00
Subscription Agency/Abonnements:
Wennergren-Williams AB,
Box 13004, S104 25 STOCKHOLM.
Tel. 08/54.12.00

SWITZERLAND – SUISSE
OECD Publications and Information Center
4 Simrockstrasse 5300 BONN (Germany). Tel. (0228) 21.60.45
Local Agents/Agents locaux
Librairie Payot, 6 rue Grenus, 1211 GENÈVE 11. Tel. 022.31.89.50

TAIWAN – FORMOSE
Good Faith Worldwide Int'l Co., Ltd.
9th floor, No. 118, Sec. 2,
Chung Hsiao E. Road
TAIPEI. Tel. 391.7396/391.7397

THAILAND – THAILANDE
Suksit Siam Co., Ltd., 1715 Rama IV Rd,
Samyan, BANGKOK 5. Tel. 2511630

TURKEY – TURQUIE
Kültur Yayinlari Is-Türk Ltd. Sti.
Atatürk Bulvari No : 191/Kat. 21
Kavaklidere/ANKARA. Tel. 17 02 66
Dolmabahce Cad. No : 29
BESIKTAS/ISTANBUL. Tel. 60 71 88

UNITED KINGDOM – ROYAUME-UNI
H.M. Stationery Office,
P.O.B. 276, LONDON SW8 5DT.
(postal orders only)
Telephone orders: (01) 622.3316, or
49 High Holborn, LONDON WC1V 6 HB (personal callers)
Branches at: EDINBURGH, BIRMINGHAM, BRISTOL,
MANCHESTER, BELFAST.

UNITED STATES OF AMERICA – ÉTATS-UNIS
OECD Publications and Information Center, Suite 1207,
1750 Pennsylvania Ave., N.W. WASHINGTON, D.C.20006 – 4582
Tel. (202) 724.1857

VENEZUELA
Libreria del Este, Avda. F. Miranda 52, Edificio Galipan,
CARACAS 106. Tel. 32.23.01/33.26.04/31.58.38

YUGOSLAVIA – YOUGOSLAVIE
Jugoslovenska Knjiga, Knez Mihajlova 2, P.O.B. 36, BEOGRAD.
Tel. 621.992

Les commandes provenant de pays où l'OCDE n'a pas encore désigné de dépositaire peuvent être adressées à :
OCDE, Bureau des Publications, 2, rue André-Pascal, 75775 PARIS CEDEX 16.

Orders and inquiries from countries where sales agents have not yet been appointed may be sent to:
OECD, Publications Office, 2, rue André-Pascal, 75775 PARIS CEDEX 16.

68236-12-1984

OECD PUBLICATIONS, 2, rue André-Pascal, 75775 PARIS CEDEX 16 - No. 43131 1985
PRINTED IN FRANCE
(81 85 01 1) ISBN 92-64-12656-2